W9-BUO-985

FIX IT FAST & EASY!

America's Master Handyman© Answers the Most Asked "How To" Questions.

Glenn Haege

Edited by Kathy Stief
Illustrated by Ken Taylor
Cover Photo by Edward R. Noble/The Oakland Press
Back Cover Photo by Gilbert Ecks
Introduction Photo by Santa Fabio

MASTER HANDYMAN PRESS

FIX IT FAST & EASY!

America's Master Handyman Answers the Most Asked "How To" Questions.

Glenn Haege

Edited by Kathy Stief

Published by:
>   Master Handyman Press INc.
>   Post Office Box 1498
>   Royal Oak, MI 48068-1498 U.S.A.

All rights reserved. No part of this book may be reproduced or transmitted by any means, electronic or mechanical, including photocopying, recording or by any information storage and retrieval system without written permission from the author, except for the inclusion of brief quotations in a review.

Copyright © 1991 Master

>   First Printing 1992
>   Second Printing 1992
>   Third Printing 1993
>   Fourth Printing 1996, revised

>   Printed in the United States of America

Library of Congress Cataloging in Publication Data.
Haege, Glenn
>   America's most answered "How To" Questions
>   Bibliography: h.

ISBN   1-880615-01-0

Trademarks:
All products, names, and services are trademarks or registered trademarks of their respective companies.

To Barbara, Eric and Heather with love.

Acknowledgments

I couldn't have done this without the help of my lovely wife, Barbara, who kept after me to get the book done, and my two great kids, Eric and Heather, who not only gave the support, but the consideration necessary, to let dad work.

This book also would have been impossible without the support of the staff and managment at WXYT Detroit, AM 1270, that have made "Ask the Handyman" one of the country's most listened to consummer information shows.

Ken Taylor, one of the best artists in Detroit (or anywhere for my money), did a splendid job of not only illustrating my words, but giving the book a feel that would make it easy to use and good to look at. My editor, Kathy Stief wrestled with my ideas, tapes, notes and scribbles, until they became the manuscript I wanted it to be. Then, all of us got together and tried to design a book that you would be proud to own.

Profound thanks must go to Ted "Mr. Hardware" Traskos, Chairman emeritus of ACO Hardware, Inc., the largest independently owned hardware chain in America. Ted had faith in me when no one but my family knew my name. His loyal support over many years, gave me the time and practice necessary to learn the craft of radio, and become what I am today. "Thanks, Ted."

Jerry Baker, "America's Master Gardener," deserves special thanks. He has been a splendid friend and mentor for many years and was one of the primary sparkplugs for this book.

Homer Formby, Joe Gagnon, Jim Kronk, Bill Damman, Jr., Rob David, Mel Small, and many others have given unstintingly of their time and specialized knowledge.

Finally, this book was really written by you. Your phone calls to my Weekend "Ask the Handyman" Show on WXYT have told me the information you want most. It has been my priviledge to answer your questions over Detroit metropolitan airwaves since 1978. My thanks. I hope you like "your book."

Glenn Haege
Royal Oak, Michigan

Table of Contents

Tip #	Contents	Page

Chapter III   Continued

Chapter IV   Floors   61

Chapter V   Furniture First Aid   71

Tip #	Contents	Page

Chapter V   Continued

Chapter VI   Exterior Cleaning & Painting   89

Chapter VII   Decks   105

Chapter VIII   Winning the Cold War   117

Tip #	Contents	Page

Chapter VIII   Continued

Chapter IX   Odd Jobs   139

Why another "How To" Book?

There seem to be about a million "How To" books out there. I believe that most of what has been written is too general.

The answers are "generic" instead of specific, as to how to do it and what to use.

With this in mind *Fix It Fast & Easy!* is the first in a series of what I hope are **really helpful** How To, or better still, "Yes you can," do-it-yourself books.

There's nothing fancy or pretencious about the book. The type is big, so that if it's a hot day and your glasses keep falling off, most of you will still be able to follow the directions. The tips have been laid out so that once you start a project, you almost never have to turn the page.

Most important, I name, names. Believe it or not, this makes this book too controversial for some book reviewers, who won't review a "How To" book that tells readers exactly what they need.

Fortuantely, this fetish for brand names is popular with readers who have made this my most popular book, and with more than 2,000 librarians, who have made my book a part of their "How To" reference sections.

My book's success, and the success of every Do It Yourself product out there, is entirely dependent upon you. You are the coaching staff, not only to me, but to all the manufacturers and retailers of the D.I.Y. industry.

Your buying power is what gets the manufacturer's attention. And they have been really listening to you. They package better, illustrate wiser, and make How To brochures easier to understand and more readily available.

The retailer is also listening. His hardware store, home center or lumber yard is more user friendly. His training programs are more often geared to serving the Do It Yourself trade than the professional builder. There is even a trade magazine called ***D.I.Y. Retailer.***

All this support gives you more reason than ever to Do It Yourself and Save. Just accomplishing a D.I.Y. project for the first time is reason enough to try it. D.I.Y. is a practical step to saving time and money. Besides, when finished, you get to brag that You Did It Yourself.

There never was a better time to start. So, Good luck, and let's get to it!

America's Master Handyman,

Glenn Haege.

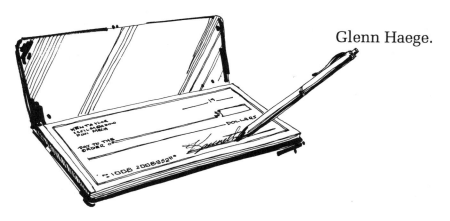

FOREWORD

My business takes me around the United States and Canada. That means I have the great good fortune to be able to speak to gardeners, do-it-yourselfers, home owners, growers, retail and homecenter operators, as well as all the professional information "handy men and women - media stars" in our two countries.

Glenn Haege has got them all beat. He has a knowledge of the subject and a way of making the "doing" easy to understand, that I have never seen duplicated. That's why I've been after him to put it down on paper for many years.

This book on home repair is terrific. The best I've ever seen. When I first saw the rough draft, I ordered a dozen copies to give my family and friends. I urge you to do the same. Every homeowner or apartment dweller, from the youngest to the most experienced do-it-yourselfer, needs one of these books.

Fix it Fast and Easy is not just a book to read and throw away. It is a tool that you will keep referring to, and that will keep saving you money for a lifetime. At the same time, it is fun to read and easy to follow. **Fix it Fast and Easy** shows you the simplest, safest and most economical way to do the job. I recommend it highly.

Jerry Baker
America's Master Gardener
August 31, 1991

WARNING - DISCLAIMER

This book is designed to provide information for the home handy man and woman. It is sold with the understanding that the publisher and author are not engaged in rendering legal, or other professional services. If expert assistance is required, the services of competent professionals should be sought.

Every effort has been made to make this text as complete and accurate as possible, and to assure proper credit is given to various contributors and manufacturers, etc. However, there may be mistakes, both typographical and in content. Therefore, this text should be used only as a general guide and not as the ultimate source of information. Furthermore, this book contains information only up to the printing date.

The purpose of this book is to educate and entertain. The author and Master Handyman Press shall have neither liability nor responsibility to any person or entity with respect to any loss or damage caused directly or indirectly by the information contained in this book.

WARNING - DISCLAIMER

GETTING STARTED
Chapter I

GETTING STARTED

1 Start With a Plan.

Put down that hammer. Don't just rush off and start banging away. Take the time to plan. This book is designed to be a good first place to look, for every home handyman and woman, everywhere. Look it up in the book and get the facts first, before you start spending time and money.

2 Get the Information You Need - FREE!

A good part of your project pre-planning is to get the factual information necessary to do the job. A resourceful D.I.Y.'er is always on the hunt, gathering How To information on a wide assortment of projects. Be on the lookout every time you go to a Hardware, Home Center or Lumber Yard. Most of the brochures and product literature sheets are **FREE.**

Bring them home and file them in one of those big, multi-sectioned manilla files you find at office supply stores. Make the section headings out to fit your interests: Inside, Outside, Plumbing, Painting, Furniture Repair, etc.

Stay away from those big, profusely illustrated How To books. They are usually not exact, or up to date enough to give you the specific information you need. Besides, **YOU CAN'T BEAT FREE!** Saving Money is the #1 reason you're a D.I.Y.'er.

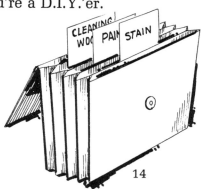

GETTING STARTED

TOOL BOX TIPS

3 Get a Tool Tote.

The big red, wheeled tool box is out of style. Light, easy to carry Tool Totes are what the D.I.Y.'er uses today because they take the tool to the project upstairs, outside, in the garage, anywhere.

I find having two Tool Totes is just about ideal. One is specially set up for light repairs and stays loaded always. The other tote stays empty until I have a specific project, then it gets loaded with everything I need for that particular job.

4 Light Repair Kit

Here are the tools I suggest keeping in the Light Repair Tool Tote:

16 Oz. Claw Hammer, Small Ruler, Cordless Screwdriver with two way bit, Locking Style Pliers, Brads, Finish Nails, Flash Light, Pencil, Stud Finder.

That's enough. Your Tool Tote is still light enough to carry anywhere and it has everything you need to cover most quick jobs.

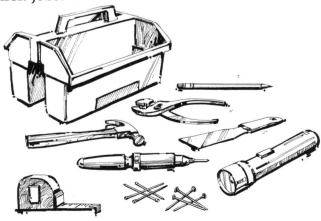

GETTING STARTED

5 Big Project Kit

Bigger projects need specialized tools. You don't need a big tote or box. Store your specialized tools in one area. Hang them on a wall, or lay them in a cabinet. Then, when you have a big job, fill your second Tool Tote with the special tools you need and carry it to the job site.

6 Stay Organized!

Neatness counts! Too many tool drawers look like junk drawers. Keep your storage area well organized and you can find everything you need quickly and easily. Let it get looking like a rat's nest and you'll be angry, tired and confused before the project is even started.

As soon as the project is completed, take your Tool Tote back to the storage area and unload it **before** you do anything else. That way your work area will be well organized and waiting for you the next time you need to get a project done.

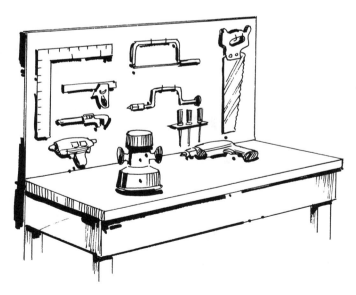

GETTING STARTED

7 Do I Really Have to Throw Out My Old Tool Box?

Of course not. But Tool Totes will really make your jobs easier. Besides, they make great gifts, so all you have to do is hint.

While you're waiting, here's a few tips on cleaning out and organizing that old tool box you've had stuck in the basement or garage for years.

1 Put a tarp on the floor and dump everything in the box on to the tarp.

2 Wipe down the outside of the box with a household cleaner.

3 Wipe down the inside of the box with a rag soaked in mineral spirits.

4 Clean off all the oil and dirt from your tools, especially the wrenches and screwdrivers with a mineral spirit soaked rag.

5 Put your tools back in the tool box in order of reverse popularity. Put your least used tools at the bottom of the box. That way, you won't disorganize your tool kit the next time you have to find your favorite pair of pliers.

6 Make certain you have a flashlight in the box.

7 Throw in a couple of pieces of chalk in the box to help absorb moisture and keep your tools from rusting; especially if you store tools in the your car trunk or van.

8 Clean off the tarp and put it and your tool box away. Now you're organized and ready for the next Handyman Opportunity.

GETTING STARTED

8 What's the Best Way to Get Extra Electric Power to My Work Area?

Usually, the work area is located in the darkest, least used corner of the basement (that's why the family let you have it). You certainly don't want to call in an electrician but getting more power is vital.

If you have to call in an electrician for any other reason, seriously consider asking him to run a couple of lines directly to your work area. Since he's already there, the extra charge should be minimal and you will have the power you need for all those electric tools you can't resist buying.

Until then, make an extension cord to fit the exact length from your nearest power source. Let's say its the plug by the washing machine. You want the exact length of cord, so that there is no surplus to trip over when you're in the middle of a project and carrying something heavy.

Making your cord is easy. You can buy heavy duty, bulk 10/3 wire cord cut to the exact length and the grounded fittings you need at your local hardware store.

While you're there, pick up a **MULTIPLE OUTLET BAR** . This unit contains six grounded outlets with a circuit fuse and a surge supressor. If you overload the circuit, you'll only trip out the outlet box, not the rest of the house.

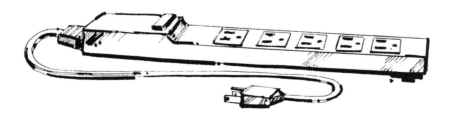

GETTING STARTED

Attach the Multiple Outlet Bar to the work bench area. Now, you've got all the plug power you need.

9 What Do I Do When I Keep Having Electrical Overload Problems?

There's no inexpensive answer. If you're constantly overloading your home's electric circuits and having to replace fuses or reset the circuit breakers, it's time to call in a **licensed electrician** and have him solve your problem.

GETTING STARTED

10 What About Face Masks?

More accidents happen in the home than on the road or in the workplace. Many of the household chemicals we use, especially in combination, can be highly toxic.

The manufacturers are listening to our needs and coming up with products to meet them. 3M's Occupational Health and Environmental Safety Division, among others, has developed lines of relatively inexpensive, highly efficient face masks, like the Easi-Air (TM) Dual Cartridge Half Mask Respirator.

This mask has special filter cartridges, such as their Model #7253, developed to filter out Chlorine, Hydrogen Chloride, Sulfur Dioxide, Dusts and Mists.

Every handy person who will use TSP and Bleach, or Muratic Acid, or any number of household chemicals, should have and use one of these masks. You only have one heart, one set of lungs, one throat. Please protect them.

One warning. Any good mask will restrict your air intake a little. Pace yourself. Don't try to do the whole job at one time or lift as much as you normally would. This is especially true if you're a little bit older, over weight or smoke.

CLEANING TIPS
Chapter II

CLEANING TIPS

TSP THE HEAVYWEIGHT CONTENDER

11 Go Out and Buy a box of TSP.

While there is no universal cleaner, Tri-sodium Phosphate (TSP) comes close. TSP is relatively low cost, versatile and very effective. It should be in every home.

In parts of the country that do not allow TSP because of its heavy phosphate content, try TSP-PF Heavy Duty Cleaner by the Savogran Co.

Warning: TSP is a generic product. Dirtex (r) cleaner by Savogran is a combination of TSP and Ammonia crystals. While this pre-mixed product is excellent, don't look at Dirtex(r) and think TSP. TSP is used with Bleach in some cleaning applications. If you do this with Dirtex the ammonia and chlorine will combine to make a poisonous gas.

CLEANING TIPS

12 Not All Cleaners Mix.

Be careful. Not all cleaners found around the house can be mixed together.

NEVER MIX BLEACH & AMMONIA The combination gives off a toxic gas that can be deadly.

Before you use any cleaner, read the instructions thoroughly. Take steps to improve ventilation before you start. Open the window, or put a fan in the room.

Chemical fumes can be bad for you. If you use a cleaner that contains Bleach or other potentially harmful chemicals get a dual cartridge face mask, like 3M's Easi-Air(TM) Dual Cartridge Half Mask Respirator with #7253 Hydrogen Chloride, Sulfur Dioxide, Dust and Mist Filters. These face masks are a little more expensive than ordinary filter masks but the extra protection is worth it.

When the job is done, be sure you store all cleaners where pets and children can not get to them.

CLEANING TIPS

13 What's the Best Way to Wash Walls?

Materials needed: TSP

Equipment needed: Sponge, Pail, Rubber Gloves, Goggles

While good for their intended purposes, many general cleaning products are not good for wall washing. They leave residues which make them unacceptable, especially when preparing the surface for painting.

Use this easy formula to make quick work out of washing walls:

Mix 4 oz. dry measure of TSP into one gallon of hot water.

Stir thoroughly with a new paint stick.

Then, wearing gloves and eye protection, wash the wall starting from the bottom and working to the top. Using a large sponge will make the job easier. Rinsing is not usually necessary but recommended.

CLEANING TIPS

14 What About Greasy Walls?

New Materials needed: 4 oz. Ammonia

• Add 4 oz. Ammonia to the 4 oz. TSP Solution. For very greasy walls, increase the amount of TSP to 6 oz..

• Use a second pail of clean water to rinse. Change the rinse water often.

• Dry with 100% Cotton Towels.

HINT: This job will go a lot faster and is a great deal more fun, if two do it together. One washes, one rinses. Make it a race.

15 What About Washing Walls Before Painting?

Use the same directions as # 13.

16 What About Kitchens & Baths?

Use the same directions as # 14.

17 What About Washing Ceilings?

Treat the same way as washing walls. Stay off the ladder. Use a sponge mop with an extension handle, like Mr. Long Arm (r). You'll get as good or better a job, and won't run the risk of landing in the hospital.

CLEANING TIPS

18 How Do I Clean Dull Ceramic Tile?

Materials needed: 2 C Laundry Bleach, 3 oz. TSP, Lemon Oil Furniture Treatment

Equipment needed: Rubber Gloves, Goggles, Face Mask, 2 Gallon Pail

If the ceramic tile in the bath has dulled from soap film build up, it's easy to make it shine. Just add 2 cups of liquid laundry bleach and 3 oz. dry measure TSP to 1 gallon of hot water.

Open the window and put the fan on. Put on rubber gloves, goggles and a face mask like 3 M's Easi-Air (TM) Dual Cartridge Half Mask Respirator. Use a large sponge to wash the tile using a lot of the mixture. Let the liquid stand on the surface 2 to 4 minutes, then rinse.

When dry, seal the tile and grout with a thin coat of lemon oil. Dry overnight before letting the area get wet.

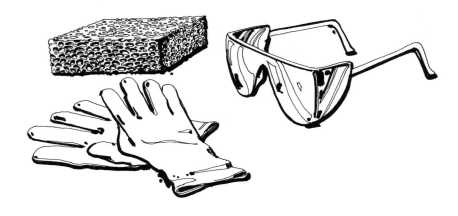

CLEANING TIPS

19 How Do I Bring Back the Luster of a Porcelain Sink?

Materials needed: Gal. Liquid Bleach, Bar of Bon Ami(r), Poly-Type Auto Wax or Gel Gloss (r)

Equipment needed: Cheese Cloth

Open the windows for ventilation. Then put the stopper in the drain and fill the sink half full with liquid bleach. Fill the rest of the way with hot water.

Let stand for 10 minutes.

Drain sink and clean with the bar form of Bon Ami (not the powder). Rinse with cold water. When dry, apply a Poly-Type Auto Wax or Gel Gloss (r) for renewed luster.

20 How About Stainless Steel Sinks?

Materials needed: Bar Keepers Friend, Waxless Lemon Oil

Equipment needed: 2 Rags or pieces of Cheese Cloth

First clean the sink thoroughly with Bar Keepers Friend(TM).

Stop future water spotting by wiping on a thin coat of waxless lemon oil furniture treatment with a piece of cheese cloth. Let dry over night.

CLEANING TIPS

21 How Do I Remove Smoke Stains From Fireplace Masonry?

There are three answers for this, depending upon how bad the problem is. Try the gentlest solution first and work your way up. You don't want to tackle solution #C unless you have to do it.

A: Light Stains:

Materials needed: Art Gum Eraser or Dry Cleaning Sponge

Light stains can be taken off by using an art gum eraser or dry cleaning sponge.

B: Moderate or wide spread stains:

Materials needed: 8 oz. TSP, 1 Gallon Hot Water, Rinse Water

Equipment needed: Rubber Gloves, Goggles, Wheel Style Tampeco Bristle Brush, Brush for Concrete Sealer, Drop Cloth

If that doesn't work, or the smoke stain covers such a large area that "erasing" it is impractical, get out your trusty box of TSP and dilute 8 oz. dry measure into a gallon of hot water.

This is a very strong TSP solution, so for the next step, use a drop cloth and make certain you have rubber gloves and goggles or some sort of eye protection.

Apply solution with a Tampeco Bristle Brush. Work the solution into a small area at a time, then rinse with clear water.

CLEANING TIPS

The next day, after the concrete is dry, seal the entire masonry area with a crystal clear concrete sealer so that the stain removal job is easier next time.

C: Very Stubborn Stain:

Materials Needed: 12 oz. Muratic Acid 20°, 1 Gal. Warm Water, Concrete Sealer.

Equipment Needed: Rubber Gloves, Goggles, Fan, Face Mask, Drop Cloths, Brush for Concrete Sealer.

Mix up to 12 oz. Muratic Acid 20° into a gallon of warm water. This is very strong stuff, so take all the precaution necessary. Clear your work area. Protect the floor and remaining furniture, with drop cloths. Make certain you have enough ventillation. Open the windows, put on a fan. You may even consider a mask to protect your nose and lungs (See Tip # 10, Page 20).

Start washing from the bottom and work your way up to the top.

Rinse the entire area with clear water when finished.

When dry, seal masonry surface with a crystal clear concrete sealer.

CLEANING TIPS

22 How Do I "Deep Clean" Oak or Other Solid Wood Kitchen Cabinets?

Materials needed: Kitchen Cabinet Creme, Mineral Spirits or Paint Thinner

Equipment needed: Sponge, Facial Tissue, Cotton Rags.

If your solid wood kitchen cabinets look dull and lusterless even though you clean them regularly, there's a good chance the problem is the cleaner not you. General maintenance cleaners just aren't adequate to get the job done in a kitchen environment.

Parker & Bailey or F. O. Bailey's Kitchen Cabinet Creme is a specialty product developed to cut through the accumulated airborne cooking residues, oils, moisture, fingerprints, and food spills. Apply with a clean, damp, cotton cloth and rub into the surface. Then, buff to the desired luster. Kitchen Cabinet Creme has no harmful or inflammable ingredients and does not contain wax, silicones, petroleum distillates or solvents which can dull and damage the surfaces, yet quickly cuts through kitchen oils and residue.

If even stronger cleaning is needed to cut through years of cooking and cleaner residue, give the cabinets a mineral spirits bath. Pour mineral spirits

or paint thinner on a sponge and wash inside and out. Remove the residue with facial tissue while still wet.

Repeat the process two or three times, then let the cabinets "breath" for four hours.

To keep your cabinets looking beautiful, apply Kitchen Cabinet Creme or light lemon oil monthly.

#23 What Should I Use for Daily Spot & Spill Cleaning of Kitchen Cabinets

Materials needed: An Organic Cleaner like Simple Green (TM), Breeze (TM), Clean Away (TM), or Clear Magic (TM)

Equipment needed: 100% Cotton Cloth

The best general purpose product for cleaning spots and spills around the kitchen is one of the new bio-degradable cleaners like Simple Green (TM), Clean Away (TM), Clear Magic (TM), or Breeze (TM). These Organics do not include petroleum distillates, and therefore do not leave a film behind after use.

One of the secrets to successful cleaning is the cloth you use to clean the soiled area. Make certain it is a 100% cotton cloth. If there is polyester in the fabric it will smear and not absorb properly during the cleaning process. Your day is too busy to waste twice the energy and get frustrated because you used an improper cloth.

It may seem that I'm wasting too much time on cleaning kitchen cabinets. I'm not, they are some of the most important parts of you house and need a lot of Tender Loving Care.

CLEANING TIPS

24 How Do I Hide Light Scratches on Formica Surface? Scratches Are Not Deep and There Is No Chipping.

Materials needed: Your choice of the following car polishes: NU-Finish®, Meguiars #5®, or Westley's Car Polish®

Equipment needed: 100 % Cotton Rag

As long as you only see the scratches when you are looking on an angle, not straight down, the following technique should work. If it doesn't, the scratches are too deep and replacement or "learning to live with the problem" may be in order.

Apply wax as directed. Let dry, then buff with a soft, 100% cotton rag. You're done!

25 How Do I Clean Very Dirty Ceramic Tile Around a Newly Reglazed Tub?

Materials needed: Gel Gloss(TM) Liquid not Spray; 4 oz. TSP; 1 cup Liquid Bleach

Equipment needed: 100 % Cotton Rags (for Gel Gloss), 2 Gal. Pail; Sponge, Fingernail Brush, Rubber Gloves, Goggles

The first thing you want to do is protect the newly reglazed tub surface. So the first thing I would do is put a coat of Gel Gloss (TM) Liquid, not the spray, on the tub. Gel Gloss is Silicone and Carnauba wax mixed together. This will give the tub surface the protection of an extra sealer to resist anything that might attack the surface. Gel Gloss will give the tub a nice glaze and make it easy to clean.

CLEANING TIPS

Then, I would call the manufacturer that sprayed my tub and ask them what's the strongest thing I can use. If they have a preferred cleaner, or sell their own product, use it. If the cleaner they recommend has abrasives in it, ask specifically if Bleach or Phosphates will be a problem.

Even though our main task is to clean the ceramic tile above the reglazed tub, anything we put on the tile will eventually get into, and attack the tub surface.

Some Tub re-glazers recommend Soft Scrub(TM) for tub cleaning. Soft Scrub is an excellent product but is slightly abrasive. A re-glazed tub's surface is so delicate that I do not like using an abrasive of any kind.

If the manufacturer says that Bleach and Phosphates are not a problem, I recommend a solution of one cup liquid household bleach, 4 oz. TSP, and one gallon of warm water.

As always, begin to wash from the bottom and work your way up to the top. Use the fingernail brush to get into the grout lines.

There are a lot of other products on the market that will do a very good job, but I recommend waiting for the manufacturer's recommendation before using anything.

After you are finished, use the Gel Gloss or any good car wax or teflon paint sealant on the walls. That will help retard the soap film build up the next time.

CLEANING TIPS

26 How Do You Clean Soap Scum Off My Shower's Ceramic Tile and Glass Door?

Materials needed: The Works Bath & Shower Cleaner (TM), Rain-X(TM)

Equipment needed: Finger Nail Brush, Rubber Gloves, Rags or Sponges

TILE SURFACE:

The Works Bath & Shower Cleaner(TM) is the secret for quickly cleaning soap scum accumulation from shower tiles and doors. This is a fairly strong cleaner so put on rubber gloves. If you are the type of person who gets your face real close to the surface you are scrubbing, put on goggles.

Start at the bottom of the tile and work your way up. You'll need a brush for scrubbing. I find the little finger nail brush you buy at drug stores effective because it has a handle and you can get in all the corners and the indentations of the grout lines.

If you have a build up or soiling problem on the shower plastic floor pan, scrub it with The Works(TM) also.

As soon as you are done scrubbing, rinse with plenty of water and let dry an hour.

When dry, give the tile surface a coat of Gel Gloss (TM).

Important: Wax the shower walls only. **Do not wax the shower floor** or it will become too slippery to be safe.

CLEANING TIPS

Glass or Plastic Shower Door

If you have a soap scum build up on the shower doors, use The Works(TM) on them also. The procedure is the same. Start from the bottom and work your way up, then rinse and let dry for an hour.

DO NOT USE AUTO WAX to protect the surface against future build up. Use Rain-X(TM). Rain-X is a crystal clear, Silicone product that is especially created for car windshields. When water hits it, it just beads up and runs down without leaving a soap scum buildup.

This automotive product has become so popular for bathroom use in recent years that the Rain-X people have come out with a product called Invisible Shield(TM) and it comes in a nice pink bottle. It is the same basic product as Rain-X(TM) but packaged differently.

So use which ever you prefer. Invisible Shield(TM) label directions say that you can use it on both the glass and ceramic tile. You can. However, using an automotive wax on the ceramic tile will get you done faster.

CLEANING TIPS

27 What's the Best Way to Replace the Old Caulk Around My Tub?

Materials needed: Liquid Bleach, Silicone Bathtub Caulk, Liquid Dishwashing Detergent

Equipment needed: Screwdriver, Utility Knife, Goggles, Rubber Gloves, old Tooth Brush, Teaspoon, small bowl or can for soapy water solution

First fill the tub half full with cold water so that the tub's structural integrity is reinforced and the tub will not settle after the new caulk is in place.

Remove as much of the old caulk as possible using a screwdriver. Cutting the caulk bead with a utility knife will help speed this process. Then wash the area with 100% (undiluted) Liquid Bleach. Use a tooth brush to scrub all the cracks and crevices real good and kill any mold or bacteria that may have found a home behind the cracked old caulk.

Rinse with water. Dry with a rag or paper toweling. Then wait until the area is completely dry (at least 1 or 2 hours).

When area is bone dry, apply Silicone Bathtub Caulk. For a professional look, mix a small batch of soapy water in a bowl or can, and smooth the caulk using the back of a spoon dipped in the soapy water.

Leave the water in the tub for at least two hours after the caulk is applied.

CLEANING TIPS

28 What's the Best Way to Get Rid of the Mold and Mildew on the Ceramic Tile and Ceiling in the Bathroom?

There are really two problems here:

First, the immediate problem

Materials needed: X-14®

Equipment needed: Cotton Rags

Spray the affected area with X-14. It will dissolve the mold and mildew in just a few minutes and you can simply wipe the area clean with a rag.

Second, the long term solution.

Materials needed: 2 Cold Air Vents

Equipment needed: Ruler, Hole Saw, Stud Sensor(TM)

Mold and mildew grow in moist, stagnent air. The small bathroom exhaust fans do nothing to eliminate this problem. The easiest way to get rid of them is to install a cold air vent over the door of your bathroom. Measure the space over the door from the top of the molding to the ceiling. If you have a height of five inches or more, you can install a cold air vent.

The two 2 X 4 s above the door are called a header. Cut the dry wall or plaster on both the inside of the bathroom and the hall side with a utility hole saw and install the cold air vents. Use a Stud Sensor(TM) to find the studs and headers. Position vents so that they are pointing up toward the ceiling, on the hall side, and down to the floor, on the inside of the bath.

CLEANING TIPS

29 How Do I Get Rid of Mold and Mildew That Has Gotten Into a Refrigerator That Was Stored, Closed, for a Short Period of Time?

Materials needed: X-14®, Baking Soda

Equipment needed: Sponge, Cotton Cloths, Baby Bottle Brush or Refrigerator Cleaning Brush

If your problem is just a small one caused by improper storage of the refrigerator for a few weeks, and you can see the mold or mildew, the solution is easy. All you need is a good deodorizing cleaner that will kill the mold or mildew on contact. One of the best I've found is a spray cleaner called X-14® that you will find in most hardware stores and home centers.

Caution: From the nature of the problem I am assumming the refrigerator is unplugged. Make certain that it is before you do anything. A supposed to be unplugged appliance, is just like a gun that is supposed to be empty. A lot of people get killed with "unloaded" guns. A lot of people get electrocuted by "unplugged" appliances.

Begin by spraying down and generally cleaning the entire surface of the refrigerator. Be sure to get all those corners on the inside. X-14® will kill the mold and mildew organisms on contact.

Once that is done, concentrate underneath the refrigerator. Take out the drip pan and wash it with X-14. Sprinkle baking soda into the pan to act as a de-odorizing agent.

CLEANING TIPS

While you're at it, take some advice from Joe Gagnon, the Appliance Doctor, and take a few extra minutes to clean out the bottom condenser area of the refrigerator. It will not only eliminate odors, it will add years of service life to your appliance.

Using a baby bottle brush, or one of the long wire handled refrigerator cleaning brushes, clean all the dust and dirt from underneath and around the condenser unit.

After cleaning the area, prop the door of the refrigerator open and let dry thoroughly (24 hours). Then, just plug in and you'll be back in business. An open box of Baking Soda stored in the refrigerator and/or freezer will absorb odors and keep the area smelling fresh.

CLEANING TIPS

CLEANING RECIPES

Window Washing Solution - Inside

2 Teaspoons of TSP
4 oz. of Amonia
1 Gallon of Warm Water

Apply with sponge. Use a squeegee.

Window Washing Solution - Outside

2 Teaspoons of TSP
4 oz. Vinegar
1 Gallon of Warm Water

Apply with sponge. Use a squeegee to remove.

WOE BEGONE WALLS
Chapter III

WOE BEGONE WALLS

30 How Do I Fill Small Holes or Cracks in Plaster or Drywall?

Materials needed: Putty Pencil, Light Sand Paper

Rub a very small hole or crack away with a pre-moistened Putty Pencil. Let set. Sand lightly.

31 What about a small hole that will have to bear weight?

Materials needed: Water Putty, Sand Paper

Equipment needed: Putty Knife

If the repairs to the wall are going to hold up something heavy, like a curtain rod or picture frame, fill with water putty.

Water putty swells. So let the job set for length of time required on label directions, then scrape off the excess before it drys. Sand when dry.

32 Should I Use the Same Materials for Larger Repairs and Nail Pops?

Materials needed: Spackling Compound, Light Sand Paper

Equipment needed: Putty Knife

Get a ready-to-use, or dry spackling compound for the larger jobs. It is not as strong, but it sands easier.

After the job has set, sand with light sandpaper folded over a block of wood.

WOE BEGONE WALLS

33 What Should I Use on Stress Cracks That Keep Re-Appearing?

Materials needed: Wall Tape like Pro Mesh(TM) or Fibatape(TM)

Cracks that keep re-appearing are usually located at stress points that have to give as your house adjusts to changing humidity and temperature conditions.

Don't fight it. Your house is bigger than you are and it is just doing what comes naturally. Instead, "bridge" the crack with wall tape specially made for the purpose like Pro Mesh (TM) or Fibatape (TM). You should be able to find some at any hardware, home center or paint store.

WOE BEGONE WALLS

34 How Do I Fix a Large Hole in Wet Plaster or Drywall?

Materials needed: Paint Sticks, Crazy Glue(TM) or Super Glue(TM), Patching Plaster, Light Sand Paper

Equipment Needed: Putty Knife

If the hole is just broken to, but not through, the lath (the wood or chicken wire backing for the original plaster job), you can eliminate the first step.

If the hole has broken through, or there is no lath, you have to create a backing support for the plaster patch. An easy way to do this is to use one of the new wooden paint sticks I keep telling you to pick up at paint and hardware stores to build a backing.

Break the paint stick about an inch wider than the widest dimension of the hole. Put a bead of Super Glue (TM) or Crazy Glue (TM) at both ends of the stick. Now push the paint stick through the hole and bring it back so that the glued surfaces touch the back of the plaster or drywall. Hold in place for a minute for the glue to set.

You can also use Silicone Adhesive or Hot Glue for this step if you prefer. If paint sticks, or other light wood is not available, cardboard may be used.

If the hole is so big that one paint stick will not offer enough support, use as many paint sticks as you need to build the backing. When you have to use multiple paint sticks, it is best to begin at the smaller areas of the hole and "build" back to the larger.

WOE BEGONE WALLS

Once your "lath" is in place and firmly set, fill the area with several layers of patching plaster or spackling compound in a stiff mix.

When the newly replastered hole is thoroughly dry, sand with a fine sandpaper folded over a block of wood.

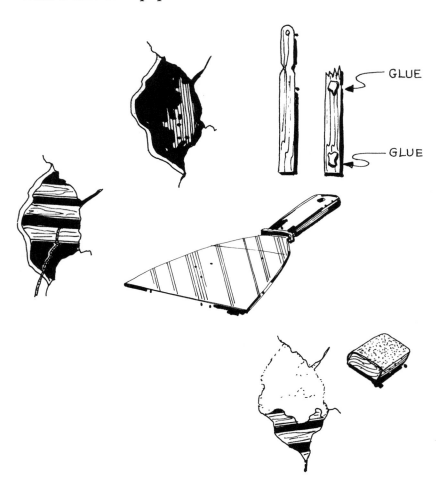

GLUE

GLUE

WOE BEGONE WALLS

35 How Do You Fix Nail Pops in Drywall?

Materials needed: Spackling Compound, Fine Sand Paper, Original Color Paint

Equipment needed: Hammer, Nail Set, Putty Knife, Small Paint Brush

Vibration, changes in temperature, or settling of the house can cause drywall nails to pop. Merely driving a popped nail back into place won't work. It will just pop back out again.

Fortunately, fixing a nail pop is easy. The most difficult part of the task will be having a smidgin of the original color wall paint on hand to "touch up" after the job is done.

To begin, drive a new nail 1 1/2" above the popped one. The last hammer blow should just dimple the surface of the drywall. Then drive the offending nail well below the surface with a nail set.

Use spackling compound to fill the dimple and nail hole. Lightly sand. Paint to match. You're done.

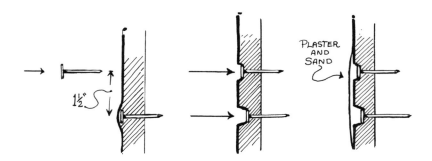

WOE BEGONE WALLS

36 How Do I Remove the Glue Remaining From Cork Squares I Took Off the Wall?

Materials needed: Old Hard Adhesive Remover (TM), Kilz Number 2 (TM) or 1-2-3- Bin (TM)

Equipment needed: Adhesive Remover Brush, Wide Putty Knife, Water Base Paint Roller & Roller Pan

If you only have a small problem area you may want to use a sandpaper screen and just sand it off. If you have a larger area, 10 or 20 sq. ft. or more, you and your wall are much better off going the chemical route.

Old Hard Adhesive Remover (TM) can be found at most hardware, home center and paint stores. It is expensive but well worth the price.

Old Hard Adhesive Remover (TM) is a strong, combustible product. Open the windows of the room in which you are working and definitely: **NO SMOKING!**

The actual adhesive removal is easy. Brush on. Wait 25 minutes. Then scrape off.

Paint the entire wall, not just the section you've been working on, with a water based stain kill, like Kilz Number 2 (TM) or 1-2-3 Bin (TM), to create a uniform surface for the remainder of your project. The stain kill rolls on just like paint and dries in an hour and a half. As soon as it is dry you can wall paper or paint immediately.

WOE BEGONE WALLS

37 What's the Best Sandpaper to Buy?

We're going to be calling for a lot of sandpaper in the next few pages. "What type of sandpaper should I use?" is one of my most commonly asked questions.

Always keep a variety of different sandpapers on hand to solve everyday problems. The type and grade of the sandpaper is printed on the back of each sheet. The numbers on the back tell you the coarseness of the sandpaper. The higher the number, the finer the finish.

The best sanding technique is to start with a coarse grade, then switch to medium and finish with a fine grade of sandpaper. This means that you need at least three different grades of each of the two common sandpapers. The two sandpapers are "Garnet" sandpaper and "Aluminum Oxide" sandpaper.

GARNET SANDPAPER: This sandpaper is light brown in color and used for sanding soft wood, drywall, fillers and patching materials.

ALUMINUM OXIDE SANDPAPER: This sandpaper's coarse side is usually a clay gray in color. It's backside may be blue-gray or pink. Aluminum Oxide sandpaper works best on hardwood and metal.

"Waterproof Sandpaper" is not usually needed by the handyman. It is black in color. The grit is made from Silica Carbide and it is used primarily for fine finishes and car paints.

WOE BEGONE WALLS

HINTS: If you are going to do a lot of sanding, or, an even surface is very important, wrap the sandpaper around a block of wood before using.

If your sandpaper gets clogged, clear the paper by sanding it lightly with another piece of sandpaper.

SANDING SCREENS: Sanding Screens are available at most hardware stores and homecenters. If your project requires sanding wall plaster, spackling compound or joint compounds, I recommend using a Sanding Screen. They cut fast and resist clogging.

When sanding with a sanding screen, use both sides. Shake the screen to clear when full. Sanding Screens come in a number of different coarseness levels and work excellently.

WOE BEGONE WALLS

38 What's the Best Way to Prepare My Walls for Painting?

Start with a plan. Make certain your working area is cleared and you have protected all adjacent areas with drop cloths.

Many people seem to think that cleanliness is old fashioned. In this case, I am old fashioned. You get the best job if you start with a clean, grease free surface, so wash the walls first. Consult the Cleaning Section of this book for easy tips on wall washing. Then make any repairs to the wall and apply a sealer coat if necessary.

WOE BEGONE WALLS

39 What Kind of Paint Should I Select for Interior Walls and Ceilings?

The type of paint you use is a personal preference. I prefer Latex paints as a general rule. For best results I suggest a "flat" paint for the ceiling and a satin or egg shell velvet for the walls. The "flat" paint on the ceiling will cut glare. The satin and egg shell will give you a harder, easier to clean surface for the walls.

Start shopping for your paint while you're still in the planning stages. Go to a your favorite retailer and don't get the "Bargain Special" unless your previous investigation has shown you that this is really a high quality paint that is specially priced.

Remember, the most expensive ingredient in your paint job is YOU. The better the paint, the better the job. A better, longer lasting job means that you'll be happy with it, and won't have to repaint for many years.

WOE BEGONE WALLS

40 How Do I Paint Over a Varnished Wood Surface?

Materials needed: 1 Cup Dirtex (TM) or TSP, Mineral Spirit Based Stain Killer, like Stain Kill, Kover Stain®, or Kilz®

Equipment needed: 2 Buckets, 2 Sponges, Rubber Gloves, Goggles, Roller & Roller Pan and Brush for Stain Kill application

Twenty years ago, varnished knotty pine and cedar rec rooms, studies and breezeways were all the rage. Tastes have changed, and many now want to paint over these surfaces.

The first thing you have to do is de-wax and de-oil the surface. To do this, make a strong, pre-painting cleaning solution by mixing 1 cup (dry measure) of Dirtex (TM) or TSP into a gallon of water. Use another pail for clear rinse water.

This is a great chore to do with another person. One person washes, starting from the bottom up. The other person rinses. Keep changing the rinse water.

Let the walls dry after they have been thoroughly washed and rinsed.

Then, coat the entire area with a mineral spirit based stain killer like Kover Stain®, or Kilz®. Use a roller and brush combination for easy application.

You do not have to take off the varnish. The stain killer has prepared the surface so that you can paint, or wallpaper right over it.

WOE BEGONE WALLS

41 What's the Best Way to Paint the Walls and Ceiling?

Materials needed: Paint of your choice.

Equipment needed: Roller and Roller Pan, 4 ft. Roller Extension Stick, Brush, Plastic Drop Cloths

Cool down the room before you start. 65 degrees Fahrenheit is an ideal painting temperature. Open the windows in the room to be painted a crack so you have good ventilation.

Remove as much from the room as possible. Push the remaining furniture to the center of the room and cover with plastic drop cloths. Protect the entire floor and the entrances to adjoining areas with drop cloths. There are sure to be some small drops and spills on these, so strong paper disposable drop cloths are preferred.

Start painting with the ceiling. If you have a 4 ft. roller handle extension, you do not need a ladder for an 8 ft. ceiling. When painting the ceiling, roll the entire width of the room. Begin by rolling out the paint in a "W" or "M" pattern. Then fill in the "W".

Use the same "W" pattern when it's time to start the walls. This gives far more even paint application than straight up and down.

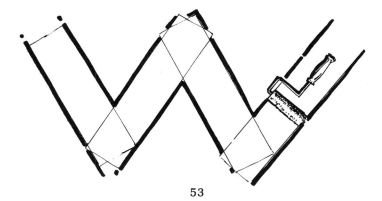

WOE BEGONE WALLS

42 How Do You Paint Over Photo Finished, Plastic Faced Paneling?

Materials needed: 8 oz. Dirtex (TM), Water Based Stain Kill like 1-2-3 Bin(TM) or Kilz # II (TM)

Equipment needed: 2 sponges, 2 pails, Rubber Gloves, Goggles, a very good Roller and Roller Tray

This is a 2 person job if at all possible. Use a very strong Dirxtex (TM) Mixture to prep the surface. Mix 8 oz. Dirtex (TM) with a gallon of warm water. The solution will be very pink. One person should wash, one person should rinse. Keep changing the rinse water constantly.

Let dry for at least four hours after washing. Then, put on a coat of water based stain kill like 1-2-3 Bin (TM), or Kilz # II (TM). Brush the paint into area's that the roller won't reach, first, then roll the entire area.

The result will be depressing. It's going to look real blotchy. Trust me. Let it dry at least two hours. Then apply your finish coat.

Two finish coats may be needed. Paint the "grooves" and other areas with a brush first, then cover the entire area with a roller.

Do not use a paint with a semi-gloss or higher sheen rate. A satin, velvet, or egg shell is perfect for this application.

WOE BEGONE WALLS

The paint you use and its application are very important. Don't expect satisfactory results using a bargain brand or by trying to stretch the paint.

1 Be prepared to pay at least $ 19 to $ 28 (1992 prices) a gallon.

2 Do not figure more than 400 square feet of coverage per gallon per coat.

3 Make certain you roll on that paint with a good roller cover. You will pay at least $4.50 for the proper roller cover.

43 How Do I Paint Over a Water Damaged Surface?

Materials needed: 2 oz. TSP, Spackling Compound, Sand Paper, Matching Paint

Equipment needed: 2 Buckets, 2 Sponges, Rubber Gloves, Goggles, Putty Knife, Paint Brush or Roller and Pan

A water damaged surface needs special attention. First, scrape all the loose paint, then sand smooth.

Next, wash the area with a mixture of 2 oz. TSP in a gallon of hot water. Rinse thoroughly.

When dry, apply a layer of spackling compound to fill the area. Let dry and sand smooth.

Finally, apply one coat of paint over the entire area. Only you will know where the water damage occurred.

WOE BEGONE WALLS

44 How Do I Paint a Wet Plaster Wall That's Peeling?

Materials needed: TSP or Dirtex (TM), Spackling Compound like One Time (TM), Fine Sand Paper, Mineral Spirit based Stain Kill like Kover Stain (TM), Kilz (TM), or X-Out Stain (TM), Paint

Equipment needed: 2 Buckets, Goggles, Rubber Gloves, Putty Knife, Paint Roller with Four Foot Extension.

Paint peeling from a plaster surface is a sure sign of wet plaster. The only way to make certain your paint doesn't peel a second time is to solve the water problem.

Usually the problem is under, or around a window. Go outside and check around the window frames. Look for loose boards or siding. Recaulk if necessary.

Inside, the problem is easy to solve. Scrape off the loose, scaling paint. Then, sand the edges. We call that feathering.

Wash the walls with a solution of 5 oz. TSP or Dirtex in one gallon of warm water. Rinse. This is a good 2 person job. Let dry at least three or four hours.

Fill in with spackling compound as necessary. A good product to use is One Time (TM). It doesn't shrink while drying like many of the others, so you only have to use it one time.

Let dry, then lightly sand any rough spots.

Finally, coat the entire area with a mineral spirit based stain killer like Kover Stain (TM), Kilz (TM), or X-Out Stain (TM). Make certain you do the entire wall or your patching job will be noticeable.

WOE BEGONE WALLS

Wait an hour and a half and repaint.

Check out my repainting tips for some techniques for making your repainting job fast and trouble free.

45 How Do I Stain Over Wood Filler?

Materials needed: Wood Fix (TM), Famowood®, Wood Patch, or Elmer's® Latex Wood Patch, Wood Stain of your choice

Equipment needed: Putty Knife, Stain Brush or Rag.

If you are going to stain over a patched area, DO NOT USE WATER PUTTY to patch the area. It will never take stain properly.

F-I-X Wood Fix (TM), Famowood®, Wood Patch and Elmer's® Latex Wood Patch are all especially made to do this particular job.

Once the patch is made, sand 'til smooth, then stain the entire area.

WOE BEGONE WALLS

46 How Do I Fix Flaking Paint and Dry Wall Disintegration Over the Bathtub?

Materials needed: 5 oz. TSP, 8 oz. Chlorine Bleach, One Time (TM) Spackling Compound, KILZ (TM) or Kover Stain (TM) Stain Kill, or Perma-White Bathroom Wall and Ceiling Paint, Sand Paper, Oil Base Marine Paint

Equipment needed: 2 Buckets, Sponges, Goggles, Rubber Gloves, Putty Knife, Rollers or Paint Brushes

Sometimes the drywall or wet plaster over a tub or shower area will become soaked from the steam and spray. Usually, the paint just starts flaking off and you know a "quick fix" is in order. Sometimes, finger size pieces of the drywall will actually start falling along with the paint.

The only way to solve this problem, is to completely seal the wet plaster or drywall surface and repaint. If your's is a one tub house, better get friendly with one of the neighbors, because this area will be out of commission for three days.

Start by taking away all the loose paint. Then, lightly sand away any rough spots. Feather sand around the edges so the old paint and spackling compound will form a flat surface.

Wash and rinse the entire painted surface with a mixture of 5 oz. TSP and 8 oz. chlorine bleach per gallon of warm water. This solution will clean the surface and kill mildew spores.

Let dry for one to two hours. Fill in the non-painted surface and any areas from which the dry wall has fallen away, with One Time (TM) non-shrinking spackling compound.

WOE BEGONE WALLS

Now coat the entire surface with KILZ (TM) or Kover Stain (TM) Stain Kill. Put on a heavy coat of this material. It will completely dry in one and one half hours.

When surface is dry, paint with an oil base marine paint. You should be able to find this at any good paint store or paint department.

ALTERNATE SOLUTION: William Zinser & Co. has just (Fall '91) introduced a Stain Kill Paint especially made for the bath, or any place (kitchen, basement, etc.) where mildew is a problem. It contains ingredients that prevent mildew growth. Zinser's® Perma-White Bathroom Wall & Ceiling Paint is both a stain kill and finish paint. Two coats and you're done.

One final thought. There are three reasons you had this problem.

1   The surface wasn't sealed. We've just solved that.

2   The hot air vent in the bathroom is partially open "cooking" the wet plaster or drywall and making it weak. Your bathroom doesn't need that much heat. Go down to the basement and close the damper on that hot air duct run.

3   You do not have proper air exchange in the bathroom. Those little ceiling exhaust fans can't really handle the job. Try installing an air vent above the bathroom door. Check Tip #28 for directions.

WOE BEGONE WALLS

47 What's the Best Way to Spray Paint Using a Aerosol Can?

You can get professional looking results when using a spray can, just by following a few simple steps.

Never spray outdoors on a windy day.

Shake the can for at least a full minute. Listen to make certain that the agitator ball is clanging freely (clear finishes do not have an agitator ball). If that ball is not moving, the paint will not be properly mixed with the propellant.

Start the actual spray operation, by testing your technique on a piece of cardboard.

Is the nozzle free and clear? Are you holding the can to close to the cardboard?

If paint starts building up or beginning to drip you are holding the can too close to the surface. Pull back to about 8 inches.

The proper spray angle is obtained by moving your whole arm across the work.

If you are going to stop for a while, turn the can upside down and spray until clear propellant comes out. Once the nozzle has been cleared in this way, you can cap and store the spray can for another "opportunity."

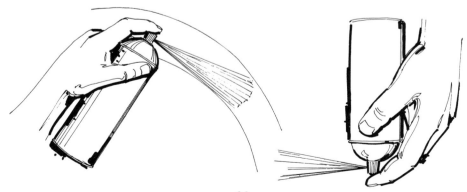

FLOORS
Chapter IV

FLOORS

48 How Do You Make Hardwood Floors Look Like New?

Materials needed: Wood Floor Creme™ or a heavy duty floor cleaner like Rennovator by Minwax®, liquid floor wax

Equipment needed: Rags or paper toweling, pail, sponge mops

Use a wax stripper to deep clean the surface, then damp mop with Parker & Bailey's Wood Floor Creme. This product hides scratches and brings back the rich, natural luster. Use sparingly, too much will make the floor slippery

Where the finish has worn away, apply Parker & Bailey's Orange Oil. Keep reapplying until the bare wood will not absorb any more. Wipe off the excess with cotton rags so that the floor does not become slippery.

If deeper cleaning is needed, use a heavy duty floor cleaner, like Rennovator by Minwax®. Wipe up. Then apply a thin coat of liquid floor wax. It's available in light, medium or dark shades. After it dries, use an electric floor buffer to bring back the shine.

FLOORS

49 How Do I Replace a Worn Out or Marred Vinyl Tile?

Materials needed: Vinyl Tile, Vinyl Tile Adhesive

Equipment needed: Heat Gun, Putty Knife, Serrated Trowel, Sand Paper

It's very easy to replace a worn or marred vinyl tile. Start by warming up the tile that has to be replaced with a heat gun. Lift the corner with a putty knife and pull up the tile.

Remove the excess adhesive from the floor by softening it with the heat gun and scraping it off.

Apply new adhesive to the floor with a serrated trowel.

Soften the new tile with the heat gun and put it down on the floor. If it doesn't fit, trim the edges with scissors for a perfect fit.

FLOORS

50 How Do I Remove Dry Adhesive From the Top of Tiles?

Materials needed: Old Hard Adhesive Remover (TM) or Weldwood Cleanup Thinner(TM)

Equipment needed: Small Paint Brush, or Paper Toweling

There are really two answers to this one:

1   If the dry adhesive is old you can remove it with Old Hard Adhesive Remover(TM). Just brush it on with a paint brush and it will soften the adhesive so that you can remove it.

2   If the adhesive is new and soft, Weldwood Cleanup Thinner (TM) will take it off.

REMEMBER: These are flammable solutions! Open windows. Bring in a Fan. NO SMOKING!

51 How Do I Brighten Up Ceramic Floor Tiles?

Materials needed: Brite (r) or Future (TM) Ceramic Tile Cleaner

Equipment needed: Mop.

If your tiles are clean, but dull, there is a good chance that is the way they are supposed to be and no amount of cleaning or buffing is going to make them bright and shiny. Many of the most beautiful 9″ ceramic kitchen and hall tiles are "single glazed," or "single fired". They were made to be non-slippery, and that means they have a non-shiny finish.

FLOORS

If you want to add a little sheen to your kitchen tiles, go to the hardware or grocery store and pick up a bottle of Brite(TM) or Future(TM). Both products contain "polymers" or "acrylics" that add a slight artificial sheen to the tiles.

Don't waste money by applying full strength. A 50/50 mixture will last just as long and add just as much sheen. Mix half and half with rinse water and apply using a cotton or sponge mop. Then forget about it. Your tiles will be the brightest they can be.

If you're still unhappy, remember that high gloss tiles and those liquid spills you always get in the kitchen could make your kitchen floor very slippery. "It's better to be safe then shiny."

52 How Do I Remove Scuff Marks From No-Wax Linoleum?

Materials needed: Waterless, non-abrasive Hand Cleaner like Go Jo (TM), D & L Hand Cleaner (TM)

Equipment needed: Facial Tissue

Scuff marks are usually a combination of black heel mark and shoe polish. To get the scuff mark off your no wax linoleum all you need is a handful of waterless hand cleaner that has no abrasive or pumice.

Rub the hand cleaner into the scuff mark with your hand until it softens the scuff.

In three or four minutes, take some facial tissue and wipe up the hand cleaner.

FLOORS

53 How Do I Remove a Shoe Polish Stain From My New Carpet?

Materials needed: De-Solv-It (TM) or Goo Gone (TM) and Facial Tissue

De-Solv-It (TM) and Goo Gone (TM) are natural style cleaners. There is no bleach in the products. However, since the products are new to you it is best to test them in an inconspicuous area before you begin the project.

Once you are certain that it is safe, dampen the fibers of the stained area with Goo Gone (TM) or De-Solv-It (TM). Then grab hold of the fibers with facial tissue and pull towards the center of the smear.

Very Important: Use facial tissue not paper toweling. Only facial tissue has the absorbency you need for this project.

Do not rub the area. Rubbing will just expand the stained area. Pinch fibers and pull the stain to the center. Repeat the process as necessary.

When the area is clean and you think everthing is gone, take about a one inch thick pad of dry facial tissue and lay it over the spot. Weigh the tissue down with a couple of books so that it is compressed into the nap of the carpeting.

Let stand for an hour, then remove and discard the tissue. This final wicking should remove the last traces of the shoe polish stain.

FLOORS

54 How Do I Remove Crayon or Candle Wax From Carpeting?

Materials needed: Paper Toweling
Equipment needed: Dull Knife, Electric Iron

Scrape as much wax off the carpeting as you can using a dull knife. Then place a dry sheet of paper toweling over the remaining wax.

Put your iron on the "Cotton" setting and iron over the paper towel working it back and forth. The warm iron will soften the wax so that it can be absorbed by the paper towel. Replace paper toweling as often as necessary.

Next time, buy dripless candles.

55 Should I Use Padding Under the Carpeting in My Basement?

Materials needed: Prime Urethane Padding

Padding does make a big difference on the comfort level when carpeting over a cement slab. It also makes the carpeting last longer. If you are going to use your basement, as a play area for the kids or a study area for yourself, padding is recommended.

Since the carpeting is below grade you have to get a specific type of padding. Ask specifically for Prime Urethane. This is padding that is made specifically for basement applications. Since it has nothing in it but Urethane content, it breaths from underneath and doesn't get mushy from the dampness.

If you want additional cushioning and warmer floors, I recommend Comfort Base (TM) by Homasote Company, a real D.I.Y. dream product.

FLOORS

56 The Floors in My House Are Beginning to Squeak. What Do I Do?

Your floor may be trying to tell you something. The #1 cause of floor squeaks is that the house is too dry. A squeaky floor is often one of the prices we pay for living in a tightly insulated, energy efficient house (You had to pay extra for this?).

If the house is too dry it's bad for the floors, it's bad for the furniture, it's bad for you. The first thing to do when the floors squeak is check the humidity level.

If it's too dry, increase the setting on the furnace humidifier and try putting an ultrasonic humidifier in the room in which you are getting the majority of the squeaks.

A couple of weeks of this humidification treatment should solve the problem. It will also make your furniture less brittle, and your sinuses will love you for it. If the humidification is right where it should be and you're still getting squeaks, try the answers for Questions 57 - 59.

FLOORS

57 The Humidity Is OK, How Do I Stop Squeaks in My Hard Wood Floors?

Materials needed: Powdered Graphite

Start the easy way. Spray powdered graphite in between the hardwood flooring where the tongue and groove boards come together. This usually does it. If not, use the "silencing treatment" for carpeted floor, listed next.

58 How Do I Stop Squeaks Under My Carpeted Floors?

Materials needed: Wood Shims, Silicone Spray

Equipment needed: Hammer or Mallet

This is a two person job. One of you goes downstairs and does the work. The other stays upstairs and walks over the floor slowly so the "downstairs person" can locate and treat the squeaks.

Bundles of wood shims are available at any lumber yard. Spray some wood shims with silicone.

The reason for the squeak is usually that there is a little too much play in the floor boards. To eliminate the squeak, you have to shore up the sub floor.

Locate the wood joist immediately below the squeak. Carefully hammer a wood shim in between the joist and sub floor to eliminate the squeak.

If the sound doesn't go away, pound in another shim beside the first one. Then go on to your next squeak.

FLOORS

59 Who Do I Sue? My Floor Still Squeaks?

Materials needed: Kant-Sag (TM) Straps, Wood Screws, or Squeak-Ender (TM) by E & E Engineering.

Equipment needed: Adjustable Wrench, Drill, Screwdriver

Don't lose hope. This final tip will absolutely, positively work. If it doesn't, check **The Exorcist** out of your local video tape store and do what you think best.

Attaching Kant-Sag(TM) straps will pull the offending flooring down to the joist and eliminate the problem.

E & E Engineering, a very innovative young company located in Fraser, Michigan, has invented and patented the Squeak Ender(TM), a little jack-like attachment that screws on to your sub floor and pushes the joist up tight against the sub floor so it is unable to squeak.

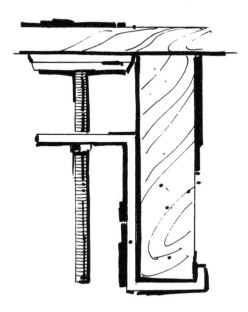

FURNITURE FIRST AID
Chapter V

FURNITURE FIRST AID

60 How Do I Remove White Rings From a Fine Wood Coffee Table?

Materials needed: White Tooth Paste, Baking Soda, Lemon Oil Furniture Treatment

Equipment needed: 100% cotton cloths

"Out, out, cursed spot."

These rings are usually caused by setting a hot or moist dish or glass on an unprotected surface. The white, cloudy rings are signs of damage to the wax build-up, not the wood.

To remove, fold a water dampened 100% cotton cloth so it fits in your hand. Squirt a three inch bead of white tooth paste on the cloth. Add 1/2 teaspoon of baking soda. Squish.

Rub the mixture back and forth with the grain of the wood. You don't need a lot of pressure. Before the surface dries, wipe it off with another cotton cloth.

Since the previously stained area is now the cleanest part of the table, it will look different. To bring back the uniform surface, mix another batch of tooth paste and baking soda and clean the wax off the rest of the surface area.

When the entire table top is clean, coat it with lemon oil furniture treatment.

Another Tip: Stop using furniture wax. Just use lemon oil furniture treatment and you will eliminate rings.

FURNITURE FIRST AID

61 How Do I Repair a Cigarette Burn on a Mahogany Veneer Table?

Materials needed: Finger Nail Polish Remover, Q-Tip (TM) or other Cotton Swabs, Stain Match Kit (if necessary), Clear Fingernail Polish, 0000 Steel Wool

Equipment needed: Inexpensive model paint brush ($ .15 to $ .35), Tooth Pick, very small mixing cup, Boy Scout Type Knife

Very carefully dab just the burned area with a cotton swab dipped in fingernail polish remover. Then, take the Boy Scout knife and, holding it flat, scrape (don't gouge) away the charred area. Use a tack rag or blow out the area to make certain that it is clear of dust.

If the wood underneath the charred area is much lighter than the surrounding surface, get a stain match kit that you can find at most hardware or home centers. Apply stain using a cotton swab.

As soon as the stain is dry, mix two drops of clear fingernail polish and two drops of fingernail polish remover. Stir with a tooth pick.

Paint two or three coats of the 50/50 mixture over the surface of the cigarette burn with a small, inexpensive artist's brush.

Let cure for three or four hours. Then polish the area with 0000 steel wool. You're done.

Next time, **DON'T SMOKE.** That way, you don't have to repair the area, and you'll be around for more home improvement projects.

FURNITURE FIRST AID

62 How Do I Repair a Small Hole in the Polyurethane Finish of My Oak Table Caused by Nail Polish Remover?

Materials needed: Varathane (TM) by Flecto, Nail Polish Remover, Carver Tripp (TM) or Gelled Wood Stain(TM) by Wood Kote, Cotton Swabs, Newspaper, Auto Polishing Compound

Nail Polish Remover dissolves the finish right down to the bare wood, so you have to restain, then build back the surface.

First, clean the damaged area by rubbing gently with a cotton swab barely moistened in nail polish remover.

Restain the surface with another cotton swab dipped into Carver Tripp (TM) or Gelled Wood Stain (TM). Use only Carver Tripp (TM) or Gelled Wood Stain (TM) because these products allow you to control the density and the porosity of the surface. They do not assume the porosity of the wood they cover like other stains. You may have to blend several different stain colors to get a color match.

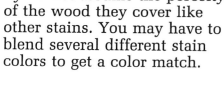

FURNITURE FIRST AID

Once the stain is dry and you're satisfied with the color, cut templates out of old newspapers that match the size and shape of the hole in the Polyurethane finish.

Put the newspaper template over the hole and spray back and forth with the can of Varathane (TM). Follow label directions. It will take several applications to gradually build the surface up to the level of the Polyurethane.

When finished spraying, let dry overnight. Next morning, you can blend in the surface with a little auto polishing compound. Important. Use polishing not rubbing compound.

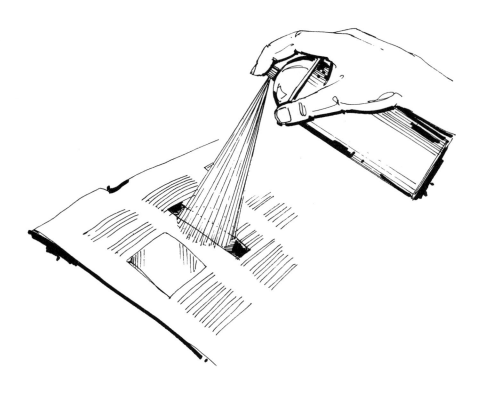

FURNITURE FIRST AID

63 What's the Best Way to Refinish Varnished Cabinets?

Materials needed: Thompson & Formby's Liquid Furniture Refinishing Kit (TM)

Equipment needed: A good comfortable pair of Rubber Gloves

Thompson Formby's Liquid Furniture Refinishing Kit(TM) is a perfect example of the manufacturer listening to your needs. Everything you need is in the kit. The products were made to work together as a system and everything, including very good, step by step directions, is there. Two different size kits are available. One is a "starter" kit for small jobs. The other is a big kit for large projects. If you're going to do a good number of kitchen cabinets, you'll need the big kit.

When doing a lot of cabinets at one time you may decide to buy your materials in bulk form after your first few kits. Be sure you buy four ought (0000) steel wool. Three ought (000) is much too rough and can ruin the surface on which you are working.

You're going to need a sturdy, yet comfortable, pair of rubber gloves for this job. Thompson & Formby sells gloves that are especially made for this project. They are thicker than the ordinary kind you find at supermarkets and are called "Refinisher's Gloves."

FURNITURE FIRST AID

Do the actual refinishing in a well ventilated area. Put plastic drop cloths or newspaper on the floors. Depending on your preference, you can work directly on the floor or on carpenter's horses. A Black & Decker Workmate (TM) worktable is also perfect for this job.

It is important to remember that with the Thompson & Formby's product you are not really stripping the varnish, you are melting it. The refinished cabinets will look much lighter than the old surface you see now.

To begin, take the doors off the frames and remove the hardware from the doors.

When refinishing, the temptation is to work too fast and try to do too much at a single time. Refinishing should be like going on a diet. You get best results when you take off a little bit at a time.

I'm not going to give you minute directions here because Thompson & Formby's instructions are very complete. Follow the package instructions and you can't go wrong.

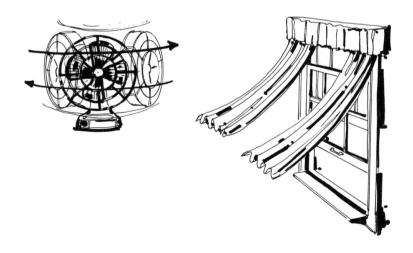

FURNITURE FIRST AID

Here are a few hints:

Don't get carried away. Work on a surface area about the size of a salad plate and go from section to section.

This is a long term project. Be prepared to use a great deal of steel wool but never throw away the solvent. It doesn't get weak, just dirty.

A section of material cut from an old pair of panty hose makes a great strainer. When you are done for the day, pour the remaining solution into a jar with a good tight top and seal carefully. Strain the solution before reusing. It will be as good as new when you begin work the next day.

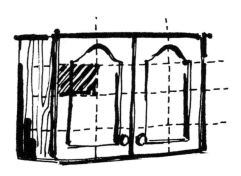

64 How Do I Refinish a Varnished Surface of Any Kind?

Materials needed: Thompson & Formby's Furniture Refinishing Kit (TM)

Equipment needed: Refinisher's Gloves

The easiest answer is to read Tip # 63 and apply it to your project. Other Varnish and Paint Removers can be used. However, Thompson & Formby's is the best all around kit.

FURNITURE FIRST AID

65 How Should I Refinish a Newly Stripped Oak Kitchen Table?

Materials needed: Denatured Alcohol, High Gloss or Semi Gloss Spar Urethane (TM), Triple Ought (000) Steel Wool, Tack Rag

Equipment needed: Varnish Brush, New Paint Stick

The best product to use to finish a "heavy use" piece of furniture (like an oak kitchen table) is Spar Urethane (TM) made by the Minwax people. This product is a combination of Urethane and spar varnish. It provides a very good looking surface that will stand up to a lot of punishment.

If the table has been standing for any length of time between removing the old finish and applying the new one, make certain that it has been thoroughly cleaned with denatured alcohol and rubbed down with a tack rag before you begin.

Brush on the first coat of Spar Urethane (TM).

As soon as it dries and you run your hand over the surface, you'll find that the Spar Urethane (TM) will have begun to raise the grain in the wood.

Take some triple ought (000) steel wool and rub down the table top to smooth the surface. Then remove the wood dust and small steel wool particles with a tack rag.

Apply a second and third coat.

Semi Gloss Spar Urethane (TM) is an excellent product but it has a stirated pigment that settles to the bottom. So if you choose the Semi Gloss Spar Urethane (TM), make certain that you stir the container every time you start a project and a couple of times during the project.

FURNITURE FIRST AID

66 How Do I Finish a Louvered Pine Interior Door? (Actually, Any Unfinished Pine Door)

Materials needed: 120 or 150 Garnet Sandpaper, Tack Rag, Wood Conditioner, Soft Wood Sealer or Pre-Stain Sealer, Stain if desired; Watco Danish Oil Finish (TM), Danish Oil by Deft (TM) or Antique Oil Finish by Minwax (TM)

Equipment needed: Saw Horses, Pad Applicator, Sponge Brush or Paint Sprayer (for advanced handy people only), Rags

This is a five step process. Remember: There are six sides to a door, four edges, a back and a front. You have to treat all six to do the job properly.

#1 It's best to use a door that has been acclimated to its surroundings. When you bring the door home from the lumberyard, don't start right away. Let it sit for at least two days.

#2 Put the doors on saw horses and lightly finish sand them with 120 or 150 garnet finishing sandpaper. This doesn't take long because they've already been sanded by the manufacturer. Just take your bare hand and rub across the surface of the door. Sand away any uneven or rough spots.

Vacuum away the wood dust with a vacuum cleaner attachment. Finish clean with a tack rag to make certain that no particles of dust remain.

#3 Apply a soft wood sealer, pre-stain sealer or wood conditioner with a sponge brush or pad applicator.

#4 If you are going to darken the wood or put on any kind of a stain, apply the stain now. Just using a rag will do the job adequately. If you have chosen to stain the wood, make sure it's dry before the next step.

#5 Apply the varnish finish coat. Get away from the brush and sandpaper and go with a wipe-down system. I recommend Watco's Danish Oil Finish (TM), Danish Oil by Deft (TM) or Antique Oil Finish by Minwax (TM).

67 How Do I Fix a Hole I Knocked in a Hollow Core Door?

Materials needed: Aluminum Foil or Paint Sticks, Water Putty, Sand Paper, Tack Rag, Oil Based Stain Kill Kover Stain (TM); Paint

Equipment needed: Putty Knife, Oil Base Paint Brush, Finish Coat Paint Brush

Remove all the splintered wood. Then, depending on the size of the hole, pack it with wadded up aluminum foil, or build a "paint stick lath" (Tip # 34, pg 44). Fill in the remaining space with water putty and smooth with a putty knife.

Once the surface is dry, sand smooth and clean the dust off the entire door with a tack rag.

Apply a coat of an oil-based stain kill to the ENTIRE DOOR, then paint with your favorite color paint. No one will know there was a hole there, except you.

FURNITURE FIRST AID

68 How Do I Finish the Sides of a New Formica (TM) Topped Oak Bar?

Materials needed: DEFT (TM) Semi Gloss, Lacquer Thinner, OOOO Steel Wool, Tack Rag, Piece of Nylon Hose to use as a strainer

Equipment needed: Bristle Brush, Wide Mouth Glass Jar

Finishing an oak bar presents a problem because it not only has to look good, it has to stand up to occasional spills and scuffs from people sitting next to it. It needs a sealer that provides a good strong protective coat.

A good product to use is DEFT Semi Gloss (TM). This product was originally made for bars, so liquids won't bother it. You'll need a minimum of three coats to give the proper protection. Deft(TM) is fast drying, so you can put on three coats in a single day. The DEFT people also make a high gloss, but using the semi gloss finish will give the piece of furniture a satiny, hand-rubbed look.

DEFT also makes another product called Deft-Thane (TM). Do not use this product for this purpose. Use the original DEFT (TM).

FURNITURE FIRST AID

Here's the technique.

Make certain you have the right tools. You need a genuine natural bristle brush, not nylon or polyester.

Begin the project by rubbing down the bar with four ought steel wool until it is as smooth as a baby's bottom. Then, carefully tack rag all the steel particles off the oak.

Apply the first coat of Deft (TM) Semi Gloss. As soon as it's dry (about 1 1/2 hours), apply a second coat.

After the second coat has dried, take the 0000 steel wool and rub down the wood again. Tack rag the surface and apply the third coat.

Here are a few tips to successful application of this product.

1- Don't try to paint out of the original can. Mix the DEFT real well, then strain it into a wide mouthed glass jar.

2- Keep mixing the DEFT (TM) while you are working.

3- If you have to stop while working, or have to stop for the day, strain the DEFT (TM) back into in's original can. When you start, the next day, mix well, then strain the product back into the wide mouth jar.

FURNITURE FIRST AID

69 What's the Best Way to Apply a Tung Oil Finish on a Louvered Oak Door?

Materials needed: Tung Oil (depending upon quantity of doors. If you are just doing one, you can use a hand applied finish like Thompson & Formby's. If you're going to do more than one door, be easy on yourself and use a brush applied Tung Oil like Water Lox(r) Transparent), Four Ought (0000) Steel Wool, Tack Rag

Equipment needed: Rags or Paint Brush, Vacuum Cleaner with Brush Attachment

This is the long, hard way to finish a bedroom or bathroom door. I personally would either paint or stain it, then add a coat of satin finish polyurethane varnish for luster and protection. The job would take one tenth the time.

However, if your interior decoration plans call for a long lasting, flat, hand rubbed look, tung oil is the only way to do it.

You will have to apply at least five coats of tung oil to finish the door properly so pick up a five pound bag of patience at your local hardware store.

If you apply the tung oil with a paint brush it will take half the time. If you hand rub Thompson & Formby's Tung Oil you will get a deeper, hand rubbed look.

Hand rubbing causes friction and develops heat, opening the pores of the wood. This allows more of the tung oil to be absorbed into the grain and cell structure. The result is a deep, long lasting finish that will never change color.

FURNITURE FIRST AID

Remember: A door has six sides. You have to finish all of them.

Begin by choosing an out of the way work area. This project will take several days. Give the door a 0000 steel wool rub down. Vacuum, then get rid of the last of the wood dust and steel wool fragments by wiping the door down with a tack rag.

Now you are ready to apply the tung oil.

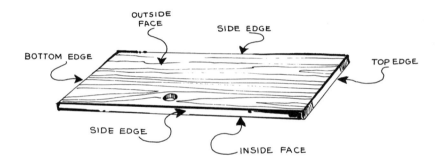

FURNITURE FIRST AID

70 How Do I Bring Back the Finish to a Baby Grand Piano?

Materials needed: Face Lift (TM) by Thompson & Formby, Meguiar's Swirl Remover # 9 (TM), Lemon Oil Furniture Treatment

Equipment needed: Cheese Cloth

Most of these beautiful instruments have a high gloss finish. Years of wax build-up have dulled the finish, not destroyed it. The finish just has to be deep cleaned. The easiest way to do this is with a product called Face Lift (TM) by Thompson & Formby.

Face Lift(TM) is a three step product. Use only steps # 1 and # 2. Step # 3 is a glaze that would not benefit your piano surface and should be discarded.

When you're done with steps 1 and 2, if you want to make the surface "just a little shinier," get Meguiar's Swirl Remover # 9 (TM) from the automotive department of your hardware, auto supply or home center. This product will take off any light scratches on the surface of the piano.

There is also a product called Meguiar's # 2 (TM). This product is a little more abrasive than # 9. It should only be used if the scratches are deeper than you can handle with # 9.

While you're at the store, pick up both bottles and read the labels, then make your decision.

After the deep clean and polish treatment, you just need a weekly dusting and cleaning with one of the many lemon oil furniture treatments.

FURNITURE FIRST AID

Moisten a wad of cheese cloth with the lemon oil and apply a thin coat to the surface of your piano and you're done. Store the cheese cloth in a zip locked sandwich bag till the next week.

Twice a year apply a thin coat of lemon oil underneath the piano. Also, keep the piano from hot air registers. A flow of dry hot air is bad for the entire piano, not just the surface.

71 How Do I Get Rid of Squeaks in Wooden Chairs and Loose Slats in Rocking Chairs?

Materials needed: CHAIR-LOC®, Paper Toweling

Squeaks in rocking chairs, and most chairs in general, are caused by the wood loosing moisture over winter. The wood has dried out and the dowel in the hole has shrunk.

The simple way to solve the problem is to pick up a small bottle of CHAIR-LOC® from your local hardware or home center and pour a bead around the offending furniture joints. The product will be absorbed into the hole and expand the wood surface to make up for the drying, and make the joints fit tight.

This problem is most often caused by dry winter air. It may also arise in older, or badly made furniture any time of the year. The solution is the same in all cases.

FURNITURE FIRST AID

72 What's the Best Way to Strip a Painted Oak Table and Chairs Down to the Original Surface?

Materials needed: Super-Strip (TM), Zip Strip (TM) or Bix (TM), Denatured Alcohol, Four Ought (0000) Steel Wool, Paper Towels

Equipment needed: Inexpensive Brush or Foam Brush, Putty Knife

If you need to take paint off of wood and want to go back to the clear wood surface, you have to be very particular about the paint remover you use. For instance, the Strip-Ease (TM) people make two paint removers: Strip-Ease (TM) and Super Strip (TM).

Strip-Ease (TM) will take the paint off, but Super Strip (TM) is needed to pull the paint pigment out of the grain. The lighter paint removers have the consistency of engine oil. Heavy duty paint removers are like cake batter.

Here's how to do it: Choose a heavy duty paint remover like Super-Strip (TM), Zip Strip (TM) or Bix (TM). Apply a thick coat of paint remover like you were icing a cake. Do not brush back and forth. Spread the remover in one direction, then go back to the can and get more paint remover. Make sure you apply a good thick coat or the paint remover will dry too soon and you won't get the job done.

After a half hour or forty-five minutes, scrape off the gook with a putty knife.

Wash the piece of furniture down with denatured alcohol and four ought (0000) steel wool. Wipe clean with paper towels. This last step is very important. You want to pull the softened pigment out of the grain with denatured alcohol as quickly as possible.

EXTERIOR CLEANING & PAINTING

Chapter VI

EXTERIOR CLEANING

73 Can I Clean Aluminum Siding?

Materials needed: Strong Telephone Finger or TSP or TSP based Cleaner and Water, or Power® or Nice N Easy®

Equipment needed: Goggles, Rubber Gloves, Car Wash Brush with Extension Handle and Ladder

This is a great question. Aluminum Siding needs to be cleaned.

The paint on millions of steel and aluminum sided houses is being ruined because they were sold as "no maintenance". Anyone with aluminum or steel siding that is more than five years old can plainly see that siding is "low maintenance" not "no maintenance."

When you get right down to it, an aluminum or steel sided house and an automobile need much the same treatment. The biggest difference is that a car has a shiny surface and gets into more dirty situations, so maintenance has to be done more often.

Aluminum or steel siding can and should be washed every year. If you do less than that, the factory coated surface will begin to deteriorate rapidly and painting will be required.

If your aluminum or steel siding is over fifteen years old before its first cleaning, repainting is probably already required.

It's a lot harder to wash a house than a car. Over the years, an entire new industry has developed to help people care for aluminum and steel siding.

EXTERIOR CLEANING

If it is in your budget, this is a good job to have professionally done. One warning: This is a new industry. No one has a long track record. Make sure you check references very carefully. Make certain that your siding does not have to be repainted before you pay for a cleaning and wax.

If you're going to have your siding cleaned professionally, the crew will come with a power generator and high pressure spraying equipment. They will use your cold water.

WARNING: THE CREW MAY BE USING VERY STRONG CLEANING SOLUTIONS.

Ask for something in writing explaining what cleaning solution is going to be used and how safe it is for plants, new grass, etc.

EXTERIOR CLEANING

Before the actual cleaning begins, make certain that your windows and all near-by furniture and equipment you don't want power washed are covered, and that nearby plants and the lawn is soaked. Dry plants may absorb too much cleaning solution and die.

IF YOU DECIDE TO DO THE JOB YOURSELF

You can use a pail, car wash brush and ladder, but I prefer power washing equipment. Power washing does a better job, eliminates the need for a ladder, makes the job a lot safer and cuts cleaning time by about 75%.

The rental company will probably stock their own recommended cleaners. It's usually a good idea to use what is recommended for the washing equipment.

If you are providing your own cleaning solution, there are many good cleaners from which to choose. TSP is an excellent general dirt remover. Mix 4 oz. per gallon of water.

If there are traces of mold or mildew on the surface, bleach must be added. When you add bleach, make certain you are not using Dirtex(TM) or any other product that contains ammonia. Ammonia and bleach combine to create a poison gas.

Siding gets hot rapidly, and can "boil off" the cleaning solution before the chemical reaction has had a chance to take place. Wash siding when it is cool, early in the morning, or in the shade. If it is an all day job, follow the sun. Clean the siding after it has cooled.

EXTERIOR CLEANING

Clean exterior walls, just like interior walls. Start from the bottom and work your way up. Don't wash in direct sunlight. If the aluminum is above brick, either wash down the brick lightly or soak it with pure water before you clean the siding.

After cleaning a section of the house, rinse thoroughly with pure water. If the clean surface is dull and lifeless, it is time to repaint.

EXTERIOR CLEANING

74 Can I Paint Aluminum Siding?

Materials needed: TSP or TSP based cleaner, Bleach, Water, Top of the Line Latex Paint,

Equipment needed: Goggles, Rubber Gloves, Power Sprayer and Generator or Sponge, Good 3″ to 4″ Exterior Paint Brush, Ladder

Sure you can. Read tip #73. It explains all about cleaning your siding. This is a very important part of the preparation for a successful paint job.

There are three main ingredients to the successful painting of aluminum or steel siding: 1- A clean, chalk free, dry surface. 2- Proper temperature. 3- A high quality Exterior Latex house paint applied at the correct thickness.

Clean siding surface as described in Tip # 73.

WARNING!

Never paint when the temperature is over 85 degrees, or under 50 degrees Fahrenheit.

It is important for the latex paint to dry slowly. Never paint on a hot, or soon to be heated surface. Always stay behind the sun and apply paint to the already cooled surface.

Select a high quality (read expensive) Latex Satin, Velvet or Egg Shell finish paint. You will probably be buying several gallons. Determine the square footage to be covered and figure 400 square feet of coverage area per gallon maximum spread rate.

Paint cans are specifically designed to store paint. That means they are filled to the very top with no room for air. Excellent for paint storage. Terrible for painting. Never paint from the bucket the paint came in. Always, pour the paint into a plastic bucket.

EXTERIOR CLEANING

It's a good idea to open and pour paint from several buckets so that you are certain to keep a uniform color throughout the job.

Paint from the top then down. Use a 3″ or 4″ Polyester exterior paint brush. The paint spreads on thick.

Do not use rapid, back and forth strokes. Apply a smooth, even coat. If you do it right, one coat looks good, but two coats will last longer.

Another application method is to use a HVLP Sprayer (High Volume, Low Pressure). Check out Krebs or Wagner Company product literature for details.

Never stretch the paint. If you're getting near the end and you are not certain that the paint will stretch, BUY ANOTHER QUART. To have a good looking, long lasting job, it is essential that your paint build to a five mil thickness when dry. Never cover more than 400 square feet per gallon of paint.

If you follow these directions carefully and wash the surface per Tip # 73 your aluminum siding will give you beauty and satisfaction for many years to come.

EXTERIOR CLEANING

75 How Do I Finish an Exterior Steel Door?

Materials needed: PBC (TM) Deglosser or Liquid Sandpaper (TM), Latex Exterior House & Trim Paint

Equipment needed: Rags, Exterior Trim Brush, Saw Horses

Steel doors can be painted outside as long as the temperature is above 50 degrees Fahrenheit. If it is a real warm day, it will be a lot better for both you and your paint job if you paint in the shade.

Prepare the door's surface by washing it down with a liquid deglosser like Liquid Sandpaper (TM).

Remember: Every door has six sides. All sides have to be painted and prepped.

Wait 15 minutes, then apply two coats of Latex house and trim paint. This will give you an attractive, yet easy to clean semi-gloss surface.

EXTERIOR CLEANING

76 How Do I Finish a New, Unfinished Exterior Wood Door?

Materials needed: Wood Conditioner, 00 Steel Wool or Light (150) Sand Paper, Tack Rag, Latex Exterior Wood Primer, Semi Gloss Latex House & Trim Paint, or Stain and Your Choice of Finish Coat

Equipment needed: Inexpensive Brush for Wood Conditioner, Trim Brush or Stain Brush, Rags and Varnish Brush, Saw Horses

An exterior wood door has both an "inside" face and an "outside" face. You may want the inside painted, and the outside stained. It's OK to finish both faces separately, but the door has to be prepped as one.

A WORD OF CAUTION:

Remember every door has six sides, an inside face, and outside face and four edges. Every edge has two side cuts at the top and bottom.

PROTECT YOUR DOOR FROM MOISTURE. SEAL ALL SIX SURFACES OF A WOOD DOOR.

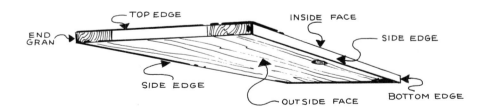

EXTERIOR CLEANING

End cuts are very important to a wood door, because the sides cuts are made up of what we call the end grain of the wood.

If the edges are not protected, moisture will be absorbed into the core of the door. Then, when the door is in use, the sun blazes down on the outside face of the door and evaporates the moisture. This heat action can easily ruin the exterior finish and may even buckle the door.

NOW LETS GET TO WORK!

Lay the door on saw horses then sand all six sides of the door with a 120 grit Garnett sandpaper or double ought (00) steel wool until the surfaces are relatively smooth to the touch.

Vacuum off the sand particles and wood dust. Dust the door carefully with a tack rag to remove any remaining particles.

EXTERIOR CLEANING

If the door is made of fir, it should be treated with a wood conditioner. Hardwoods, like Oak, Ash or Aspen, are naturally dense and do not need a wood conditioner.

If you are going to stain the door, or stain the outside face of the door, do that project first.

Over stain the door just like you were painting. Then, when the stain starts to look dull and dry, take rags and wipe the door until you get the color you want.

Let the door dry completely before applying your choice of finish coat. I would use a spar type varnish. Thin the first coat 20% with turpentine.

It's best to apply three coats of varnish. Be sure to apply the finish coat to all four edges of the door so that you seal the door against moisture.

If the complete door, or the inside face of the door is going to be painted, apply a primer coat. A water base stain kill like Bull Eye 1-2-3®, or X-Out (TM) is excellent for this purpose.

Your primer or base stain coat should dry in about two hours, so take a short break, or do another chore.

If you have prepped your door properly, one finish coat of paint will be all you need. I suggest a Latex House & Trim Paint for the finish coat. This will give you an attractive, yet easy to clean, semi-gloss surface.
Remember to flow the paint on. No choppy strokes.

EXTERIOR CLEANING

77 How Do I Save a Wood Exterior Door That Is Beginning to Ripple When It Is Too Cold to Take the Door Down and Refinish It?

Materials needed: 3 M Coarse and Fine Grit Sanding Pads, Waterlox Transparent (TM)

Equipment needed: Rags

 **IMPORTANT: THIS IS A FIRST AID MEASURE, NOT A FIX. THE FIX IS EXPLAINED IN TIP #78.**

When exterior doors are not finished properly, moisture enters the wood at the edges, and destroys the exterior finish as it is drawn out by the sun.

As soon as the exterior finish is gone the outer surface of the door begins to ripple or, in very bad cases, the door buckles.

Naturally, this usually happens when it is too cold, or too hot, or you are too busy to do anything about it.

This First Aid measure can be applied in almost any weather and should save the door until you have the time, or the right weather conditions, to refinish the door.

If it is winter, do this work in the "heat of the day", when the door will get the most exposure to the sun. Sand down the surface and edges somewhat with 3 M sanding pads. Start with a coarse pad and then finish with a fine pad. The pads are much better than sand paper for this job so they are worth the slight extra cost.

EXTERIOR CLEANING

When the sanding is finished, dip a rag in the Waterlox Transparent (TM) and rub it into the wood.

Waterlox (TM) is a tung oil varnish and will seal and protect the surface. Try to get the wood outside face and all four edges of the door to absorb as much of the Waterlox Transparent (TM) as possible.

Let the door dry overnight, then come back the next day and put on a second coat.

I've saved doors with this technique when it was as cold as 10 degrees Fahrenheit outside. It should work for you.

As soon as you have time, or the weather conditions are good, refinish the door using the directions in Tip # 78.

EXTERIOR CLEANING

78 How Do I Refinish an Exterior Wood Door That Is Beginning to Ripple and Split?

Materials needed: Varnish Remover, Denatured Alcohol, Mineral Spirits, Coarse, Medium and Fine Sandpaper, Wood Filler, Exterior Wood Finish of your choice

Equipment needed: Screw Driver, Inexpensive Varnish Remover Brush, Putty Knife, Vacuum Cleaner with Attachments, Saw Horses, Exterior Finish Brush

Take the door off its hinges and lay it on saw horses. If the exterior face of the door was varnished and enough remains on the door, take it off with varnish remover. Layer the varnish remover in one direction like icing a cake. Scrape off with a putty knife. Then wash the entire door down with denatured alcohol.

EXTERIOR CLEANING

If large cracks are visible, fill them with a latex wood filler like Dap(TM) or Wood Epoxy.

Sand all six surfaces of the door smooth. Depending on the condition of the door, begin sanding with a rough, or a medium grade sand- paper then change to a 150 grade of sandpaper. Vacuum, then wipe the last of the sanding dust away with a tack rag.

If you are going to re-stain and varnish, wash the door down again. This time, use mineral spirits.

In most cases I would refinish the door with paint. This is especially true if you had to fill some splits with wood filler, or the door surface was covered with a veneer that has begun to ripple or split.

If you are painting the door, apply a coat of exterior oil base primer and two coats of a Latex Semi Gloss Exterior House and Trim Paint.

EXTERIOR CLEANING

79 How Do I Restore T-111 Siding?

Materials needed: RestoreX® Wood Cleaner

If your T-111 has blackened and weathered, you can clean away those spots with a product called RestoreX® Wood Cleaner that you will find at many hardware stores, home centers and lumber yards.

Restorex (r) also makes an exterior paint remover that comes in the same size can, so make sure you bring home the right product (as you can tell, I've been in a hurry and grabbed the wrong one on a couple of occasions).

Restorex® Wood Cleaner comes in a jelly form. Spread it on the stained or blackened area and it will gradually pull out the discoloration.

Two words of caution: First, Restorex® is an extremely slow acting product, so you can't be in a hurry. Just spread it on and let it work. Second, the product needs heat for the chemical reaction to take place. The best time to use Restorex® is in the late spring and summer. Never when the daytime temperature is under 60 degrees.

When the T-111 is back to white wood again, I suggest the application of a solid latex stain. Don't scrimp here. Buy only first quality goods.

GETTING ALL DECKED OUT FOR BACKYARD FUN

Chapter VII

DECKS

80 How Do I Protect My New Wolmanized (TM), Wolmanized Extra (TM), Lifewood (TM) or Other Pressure Treated Wood Deck?

Materials needed: Seasonite (TM) by the Flood Company or Wolman (TM) Cedar Toner

Equipment needed: Roller and Pan or Garden Sprayer

The key to a long lasting pressure treated deck is keeping the wood cell structure supple so that water movement and evaporation does not split the wood.

All Womanized (TM), Lifewood (TM) or other pressure treated woods contain a CCA (Chromated Copper Arcinate) and water solution that has been pumped into the wood under tremendous pressure.

If left to dry normally the Wolmanized (TM) wood will split as the water finds the weakest part of the board and makes its escape.

The Flood Company has developed a special product called Seasonite (TM) that soaks into the wood and helps keep the fibers of the wood supple, minimizing the stress of structural cracking.

Seasonite (TM) should be applied as soon as the lumber is cut or the deck built. In fact, you might want to treat the timbers and deck boards before construction begins. Then finish off the top and edges of the deck and all freshly cut wood, after it has been built. This product was designed to perform on moisture laden lumber, so do it right away for best results.

Wolmanized Extra(TM) already has a waterproofing product added. No Seasonite(TM) is needed.

DECKS

81 How Do I Prepare My Deck For Sealing?

Materials needed: Acid based deck brightener

Equipment needed: Garden Sprayer, Pressure Washer, Gloves, Goggles, Old Pair of Pants

To learn all the whats, whys and wherefores of proper deck cleaning and care I recommend you read my *Complete DECK & PAVER GUIDE*. However this is enough information to make your deck look twice as good as the one next door.

Work in the cool of the day. Water down shrubs and flowers thoroughly. Mix up a couple of gallons of a good acid based deck brightener such as Flood® Dekswood®, Cabot® Stains Problem Solver® Deck Brightener, Wolman® Deck Brightener, Cupernol Revive® Easy Deck Cleaner or Performance Coatings Weatherblaster® in a garden sprayer.

This is strong stuff. Protect yourself with goggles, gloves and skin-covering clothing. Spray on the deck brightener and let it work according to the product directions.

Rinse off the solution with a strong stream of water. If the deck is just beginning to gray, you can use a water hose. If the wood has strongly greyed, use a pressure sprayer. Keep the pressure between 800 and 1000 PSI so that you do not gouge the deck wood.

The deck must dry 48 (rain-free) hours before sealing.

DECKS

82 Does My Deck Need to Be Sealed?

Materials needed: Clear Wood Sealer by Thompson, Cabot, Olympic and many others.

Equipment needed: Paint Brush, Roller or Low Pressure Sprayer

All soft wood decks like Pressure Treated (Wolmanized (TM), Lifewood (TM), etc.) pine should be sealed within thirty days of construction to help prevent cracking, cupping, nail pops and knot holes. They should then be resealed every six to twelve months. Sealing will darken the wood sightly.

The importers of the ultra-high quality hardwood decking materials (Jarrah, Ipe, Balau, etc.) assure us that these very strong woods do not ever have to be sealed because of their dense cell structure. Historically, these naturally insect and rot resistant hardwoods last five or ten times longer than softwoods, so they are probably right.

If you have a softwood deck like Redwood, Cedar or Pressure Treated Pine, the best way to seal it is with a roller using a 4 foot extension handle, or one of those power rollers that attach right on to the sealer container. Some manufacturers recommend low pressure garden sprayers.

Use a paint brush to apply the sealer to the rail system, then seal the deck with a roller, finish the stairs with a paint brush. Place a section of cardboard under the railing to catch drips on the deck.

Professionals often use power spraying equipment. If you choose to use a garden sprayer, make certain that you do not "puddle" the product and be very careful not to kill the surrounding foliage with overspray.

DECKS

To help prevent plant damage take the following precautions:

1　Soak the surrounding ground and plants with water before you seal.

2　Cover sensitive greenery and flowers with drop clothes.

3　Apply sealer to the railing and stairs with a paint brush.

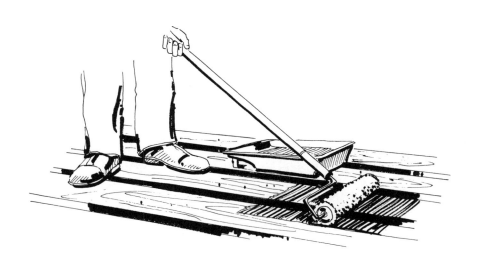

DECKS

83 How Do I Prevent My Deck From Graying?

Materials needed: Clear UV Sealer/Protectors like Dap's Wood Life Premium (TM), Cabot's Clear Solutions (TM), Sikken's Cetol Deck (TM), Thompson's Wood Protector (TM), or Penofin (TM)

Equipment needed: Roller & Paint Brush

Under normal conditions any kind of wood deck, softwood or hardwood, sealed or unsealed, will turn gray in one to eight months. If you like the gray color, and many people prefer this look, just seal the softwood deck every half year. You need do nothing if you have a premium hardwood deck.

Graying of a deck is caused by two factors: The big culprit is the ultra violet rays of the sun which kill the top layer of wood cells. A secondary factor is mold and mildew.

If you want to retain the natural color, or at least slow down the graying, of your deck, you need to apply a sealer that contains an ultra violet screener and a mildew inhibitor.

Name brands include: Dap's Wood Life Premium (TM), Cabot's Clear Solutions (TM), Sikken's Cetol Deck (TM), Thompson's Wood Protector (TM), or Penofin (TM).

CAUTION #1: These UV Sealers will all darken the deck to a honey nut color and will show traffic patterns as the surface protection is worn off by floor traffic.

DECKS

Both the Wolman Company and CWF have created Toner Sealers that both seal and cover up the green color of pressure treated wood. The Wolman product is called Wolman Cedar Toner (TM). The CWF product is called CWF-UV-Cedar.

Many of the hardwood deck people recommend using combinations of linseed oil and mineral spirits on their decks. This will not be absorbed into the dense cell structure of the hardwood. I recommend professionally prepared products like Sikken's Cetol Deck (TM) and Penofin (TM).

CAUTION #2: Whichever way you decide to go, read the labels carefully. Some products, like Thompson's Water Seal (TM), are one coat products. Other UV Sealers, like C.W.F. (TM) by the Flood Company, are two coat, wet coat products. You have to apply the second coat before the first coat has dried. READ CAREFULLY!

DECKS

84 My Deck Is Old and Grayed. Can I Stain It?

Materials needed: Cleaning Supplies, Deck Stain

Equipment needed: Scrub Brush, Hose & Water, Roller with Extension Handle, Stain Brush

You sure can. This is another great example of manufacturers listening to what the consumer says he needs and going out and making it available to him. The Cabot, Olympic, and many other companies are coming out with special deck stains.

Keep these points in mind.

1   Start with a clean deck. For most decks you can use a 4 oz. dry measure TSP to a gallon of water for the cleaning solution. Apply the solution generously. Let it stand for a few minutes. Then, wash off with a garden hose.
    If your deck has really darkened over the years, follow my bleaching directions, Tip # 81.

2   Let the deck dry for at least 48 hours between cleaning and staining.

3   Be sure to use an especially prepared deck stain. Regular wood stains will not hold up to the foot traffic.

4 Read the label thoroughly. See if the stain includes a mildicide and water repellent. If not, you will have to seal in a separate application after you have stained the deck. In the Midwest, it is always good to add Stay Clean (TM) mildicide additive to the sealer, even if it says a mildicide is already included.

We need the extra protection!

This is a great Friday evening project when the family will be away all weekend. Let the deck dry at least 2 days before walking on the surface. It probably won't take that long to dry, but you don't want to risk tracking stain into the house and on your carpeting, etc.

Remember, a stain is always darker than the original finish. Once you start staining, annual maintenance will be needed because the traffic patterns receive more wear and will be plainly visible.

DECKS

85 Can I Treat a Redwood Deck Like an Ordinary Softwood Deck?

Materials needed: Oxalic Acid Crystals, Laundry Soap

Equipment needed: Long Pants, Long shirt, Goggles, Rubber Gloves, Scrub Brush, Pail and Garden Hose

The answer to this question is "No," "Yes," "No," "Yes."

The first "No." The natural tannins that give Redwood its beautiful red color react with water to form Tannic Acid. This in turn reacts with the iron in nails to form black streaks. So if you build a Redwood Deck it is best to use stainless steel nails.

The first "Yes." If you want the redwood to weather naturally, just leave it alone and it will become a very nice "silver" color in one to two years.

I have to thank a young friend of mine, Eric Stief, for the second "No." Redwood reacts differently to cleaners than ordinary softwood. Eric spent an entire summer researching the best way to "bring back" redwood once it has begun to discolor. Here's Eric's recipe.

NEVER USE TSP ON A REDWOOD DECK!

"Never use TSP on a redwood deck. It reacts with the chemicals in the wood to form an ugly red/brown/puce color. If you just want to clean the surface, use ordinary laundry detergent.

DECKS

Most common Redwood Problems.

"Most homeowners have two problems with redwood: Black Spots and "Graying." Normal cleaning will not solve either of these problems.

"The best way to "rejuvenate" a redwood deck and clear away its gray and black spots, is to give the deck an Oxalic Acid bath. This is like giving the deck a "Facial Peel." The Oxalic Acid eats away the top cell layer leaving an entirely new cell surface."

You can find Oxalic Acid Crystals in many hardware and paint stores.

DANGER !

Like all acids, Oxalic Acid is dangerous. Extreme care must be taken. Protect your eyes, hands and skin. While working, the deck is "off limits" to everyone: spouse, kids and pets. They can all get serious burns.

DECKS

Super saturate the surrounding grass and all plants with water before beginning.

The process itself is simple:

1   Sweep and spray wood down with a garden hose.

2   Scrub wood with a solution of 1/4 cup laundry detergent to 1 gallon of water.

3   Rinse wood thoroughly with a garden hose.

4   Immediately apply a light coat of Oxalic Acid Solution. Be sure to put on your long pants, shirt, goggles and gloves for this part.

The solution can be 1 to as much as 4 oz. of Oxalic Acid crystals to a gallon of water. Use as weak a solution as possible. Experiment with a 1 or 2 oz. solution and see if that gets the job done. If not, use a stronger solution.

5   Allow the acid to dry on the wood.

6   Rinse wood thoroughly.

7   Let dry 24 to 48 hours and seal immediately.

The final "Yes." You can use regular sealers on redwood. Thompson's Wood Protector (TM) or one of the other premium sealers that include both a UV Blocker and a Mildicide work great.

WINNING THE COLD WAR
Chapter VIII

WINNING THE COLD WAR

86 What's the Best Way to Save on My Heating Bills?

Materials needed: Checkbook

Equipment needed: Telephone

The four most economical ways to save money on heating bills are:

#1 Get an Energy Audit. An Energy Audit will tell you where your greatest heating losses are and the most economical ways to save heating dollars. Best of all, they are free from many utility companies. You can't beat the price, so make it a priority to call your utility company and get more information.

#2 Get a Set Back/Set Up Thermostat. Set Back/Set Up Thermostats adapt your house's temperature to your family's needs. They warm the house when the family wants it warm and let the temperature drop when the lower temperature won't cause any inconvenience. If you have air conditioning, they will save you even more money during the summer than they do in the winter.

Good Set Back Thermostats cost from $39 to $79 so don't pay more. You can get them at any good hardware or home center. Three of the best manufacturers are: Honeywell / Magistat, White Rogers and Hunter. This investment will pay for itself in the first year.

WINNING THE COLD WAR

#3   Get a Portable Humidifier. Most furnaces send heat that is too dry into your home. Dry heat isn't healthy for either you or your house. If you've ever been to Arizona, you know that hot, dry air does not feel as warm as moist heat. Putting the proper amount of humidity into your home will make you feel warmer at a lower temperature.

If you want to make certain your house has enough humidity, buy a hygrometer or humidity gage. You can get one for about $ 7.00 at most hardware stores or home centers. With the hygrometer you can test each room individually for humidity and use your portable humidifier to get exactly the humidity you need for maximum comfort, savings and health.

Adding proper humidity also pays a big dividend in health and comfort. Dry air is bad for the skin and sinuses. Proper humidification makes you feel better.

#4   Add Attic Insulation. Most of your heat loss is through the attic of your home, so one of the best investments you can make to save money on heating bills, is to make sure you have enough attic insulation. If you add enough insulation so that the combination of the old plus the new adds up to a depth of 12 inches, your house ceiling will have an R Factor of 38. This is more than enough for most houses in the USA. Don't forget: When you insulate, you must ventilate.

WINNING THE COLD WAR

87 Some of My Rooms Are Hot, Some Cold. How Do I Heat the House Evenly?

Keeping every room in the house warm is easy if you follow these tips.

1. Balance the heat in each room by going down into the basement and adjusting the dampers in each duct. Ducts leading to small rooms, like bathrooms, should be dampened down. Ducts leading to major rooms, like the family room, should be wide open.

2. Install register air deflectors to keep the air current closer to the floor.

3. If you still have a problem "cold room", install a hot air duct booster going to that room.

4. Make sure you have proper humidity. Proper humidity levels will keep you warm without turning up the thermostat.

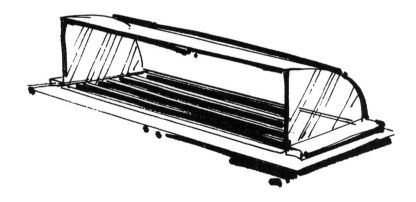

WINNING THE COLD WAR

88 What Do You Use Air Deflectors for?

Air deflectors are those cute little things we step on in the middle of the night and crack. Actually, they can be very handy yet inexpensive pieces of equipment.

Although there are now some unbreakable air deflectors on the market, the majority are made of plastic and cost only about 90 cents. They are very easy to install because they are magnetic. All you have to do is unwrap them and place them over the hot air and cold air return registers.

Air Deflectors have two uses. Placed over hot air registers, they direct the heat down to the floor, so your feet stay warm and you get more use out of your heating dollar.

The second use is to protect your furnace from being sabotaged by your curtains. Many homes have registers located under windows hung with long sheers which actually cover the registers. If they cover a hot air return, they keep the heat from circulating through the room and direct it up toward the ceiling. Installing an air deflector in this case directs the heat down and away from the sheers.

If the curtains are hung over a cold air return, the material often gets sucked into the register and blocks the register when your furnace turns on. This starves your furnace for air. Installing air deflectors, keeps the curtains pushed away from the register and lets your furnace "breathe".

WINNING THE COLD WAR

KEEPING THE WIND OUT OF WINDOWS!

89 How Do I Fix Drafty Windows?

Materials needed: Butyl or Silicone Caulk, Shrink To Fit Plastic Window, TSP, and Bleach.

Equipment needed: Candle & Matches, Putty Knife, Bucket, Gloves, Bucket, Sponge.

It's easy to stop wasting energy through drafty windows. You can locate the most drafty windows in your house by moving a lighted candle all around each window frame on a windy day. The flickering candle flame will show you where the air is leaking. Be extremely careful. Do not let the candle flame come in contact with curtains, sheers, or any other flammable objects.

To stop the leak, inspect the caulking and glazing on the outside of the window for cracks and dry-out. Replace the cracked and dried caulk with a Butyl or Silicone caulk. Replace old, cracked glazing with new glazing.

WINNING THE COLD WAR

For maximum energy savings, use an inside plastic window. The shrink-to-fit style is highly recommended. Wash the windows with a solution of 1/2 cup of bleach, 1 1/2 oz. TSP and a gallon of water, and let dry thoroughly, before you seal the windows.

P.S. You can re-use Shrink-To-Fit windows up to 4 seasons.

90 What's the Best Way to Take Off Old, Hard Putty?

Equipment needed: Heat Gun with Putty Shield, Large Screwdriver.

The best way to take out old dry putty from around windows, without cracking the window panes, is to use a heat gun with a putty shield on the nozzle. Set the heat gun on high. This will make the putty soft in a very short time and you can just scrape it away with your screwdriver.

Brookstone Stores and catalogues also stock a special putty remover tool that hooks on to an electric drill bit. If all else fails, try that.

After you've scrapped away the old putty, wash the area with a rag soaked in Paint Thinner before applying new putty. If the wood is not painted, brush on a coat of Penetrol(r) by the Flood Company.

WINNING THE COLD WAR

91 What's the Best Caulk to Use Around Windows and Cracks Outside?

Materials: Acrylic Latex Caulk, Backer Rod
Equipment needed: Caulking Gun

Acrylic latex caulk is the best basic caulk for around the house. Be sure to cut the barrel on an angle so that you get about a 3/8″ bead. Each tube will give you 18 to 20 feet coverage.

Before you start to caulk, you can stick an awl down the barrel to puncture any seal that might have developed during storage.

While you're caulking, if you come to a crack that is deeper or wider than 1/2″, fill it with backer rod first, then caulk over. This will save you a lot of time and caulking compound.

When you're finished, just slide a long nail in through the barrel and store for next time.

WINNING THE COLD WAR

92 What's the Best Way to Replace Dried Out Window Putty?

Materials needed: Glazing Compound
Equipment needed: Glazing Knife

It's your choice. You can use either the traditional bulk glazing compound or use the new Place N Press style.

The traditional method is less expensive. Just roll the material into a thin strand in your hand, place the strand down on the track and shape with a glazing knife.

The new Place n Press style glazing material is faster, neater but more expensive. It comes on a roll. Since it is already measured, you just place it down and shape into place with your glazing knife.

WINNING THE COLD WAR

93 How Do I Correct Windows That Frost Up?

Materials needed: U-Strip Draft Seal, Stretch to Fit Outside Windows, or Shrink to Fit Inside Windows.

Equipment needed: Scissors or Razor Blade

If your windows form frost on the inside each winter, they are adding money to your heating bill. To eliminate the frost:

1　Read the amount of humidity in the room. If it is too high, increase the air circulation.

2　Properly weatherstrip the window using U-Strip draft seal. U-Seal works better and lasts longer than foam tape style products.

3　Add Shrink to Fit Plastic Windows on the Inside, or Stretch to Fit Windows on the Outside.

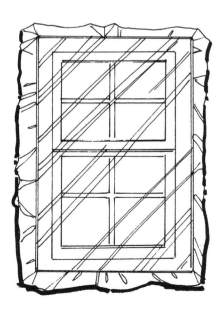

WINNING THE COLD WAR

94 I've Caulked and Re-Glazed My Windows. Now I'm Getting Condensation on the Inside of My Second Story Storm Windows. How Do I Eliminate It?

Unless the condensation is really bugging you, you should live with it. The condensation is telling you that you did a good job. The storm window is creating a thermal break. The only thing you could do to improve upon the situation, would be to change the glass in your inside windows to low emissitivity (Low E) glass that is especially made to lessen the effects of the sun.

This would increase the R factor of your interior window lowering the temperature inside the thermal barrier created by the storm windows.

The reason that you're having a problem with the second story windows and not the first story windows has a lot to do with what we call the "thermo conductivity" of the building, and also what we call a "convection loop".

The heavier, colder air stays on the bottom and the lighter, hotter air rises to the top. you have more air flow downstairs, because your hot air registers have more cubic feet of air mass blowing through the downstairs registers than the upstairs. Also, more warm air leaks out through the glass panes upstairs than downstairs.

127

WINNING THE COLD WAR

95 I Don't Have Storm Windows, What's a Good Replacement?

There are three good alternatives to storm windows for older, single frame interior windows.

1. The best is a plastic, magnetic interior storm that snaps into place. It's permanent. You can clean it. And, it acts as a real sound deadener. Cutting down on outside noise as well as drafts.

2. Shrink to Fit Inside Plastic Windows.

3. Stretch to Fit Exterior Plastic Windows.

Both 2 and 3 are effective, but are rather delicate and have to be replaced every year or two.

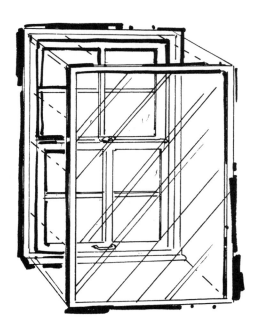

WINNING THE COLD WAR

96 How Do I Apply Shrink to Fit Interior Storms?

Materials needed: 3 M or equivalent Shrink To Fit Interior Storm Window Kit

Equipment needed: Razor Blade, Ruler, Electric Hair Drier/Blower

I recommend 3 M Kits because they have a special "repositional" tape inside that has been especially created to not pull off paint when you take the window down. The 3 M people worked for three years to develop this tape so it is the best that modern technology can deliver. However, there is always a possibility that some paint will be lifted when you take the windows down.

The actual installation is easy. Just follow the directions on the bottom of the box. I use a razor blade and yardstick to trim the sheet to the exact size I need. However, be sure you do the following.

1 Never tape the tape to the window glass. You have to create a dead air space between the glass and the plastic sheeting to make the buffer effect to keep the cold out. Tape the plastic shrink wrap to the outer edge of the window frame along all four sides. If the frame is imbedded in the wall, tape the plastic sheet to the wall.

2 Put your electric hair drier on warm and "blow dry" the plastic sheet until it forms a perfectly tight, almost invisible shield.

If you are careful with these windows, you can take them down and use them for several seasons. That makes them a very cost efficient storm window for your home.

WINNING THE COLD WAR

97 Is Any Window Preparation Necessary Before Adding Interior Storm Windows?

Materials needed: 1 1/2 Oz. Dry Measure TSP, 4 Oz. Ammonia, 1 Gal. Warm Water

Equipment needed: 2 Gal. Bucket, Sponge, Beach Towel, Squeegee

Make sure you wash your windows before putting up any type of interior storm windows or you might start growing a mold garden.

Add 1 1/2 Oz. Dry Measure of TSP and 4 oz. liquid Ammonia to a Gallon of warm water. Roll up a beach towel that you are no longer using, and put it on the sill at the bottom of the window you are going to clean. This will absorb any stray drops of cleaning solution.

Apply the cleaning solution with a sponge. Squeegee the cleaning solution off with a live, rubber squeegee. Wipe up the excess water with the bath towel.

As soon as the windows have dried thoroughly you can install your interior storms.

WINNING THE COLD WAR

98 Do They Have Temporary Windows for the Outside?

Materials needed: 3M Stretch To Fit Exterior Window Kit.

Equipment needed: Razor Blade and Ruler for Cutting.

3 M makes an exterior "stretch to fit" window. It is effective, but I do not recommend it as highly as the interior windows because it is not as neat in appearance and only lasts one season.

The directions are plainly laid out on the back of the package. I'd use a razor and yardstick or ruler for trimming the plastic sheet to size.

Two "clutz" cautions.

#1   Make sure you use this on the outside only. Inside and outside 3 M kits are not interchangeable.

#2   You have to pick a perfectly calm day to install this or the sheeting could blow and get so wrinkled you will have to throw it away.

WINNING THE COLD WAR

99 My House Gets Too Much Humidity in the Winter. What Should I Do About It?

Materials needed: Piece of kite string, roll of Tape, Dedicated Furnace Air to Air System

Usually when a home has too much humidity during the winter time, it is a sign that the furnace is not getting enough air. To test this out take a piece of kite string and tape it to the molding above a window.

Make certain that all the windows and doors are tightly closed. Then wait until the furnace goes on.

After the furnace has been on for about two minutes, open the window. If the kite string goes outdoors, against the screen, you have a positive air pressure and do not have to do a thing.

If the kite string blows in, you have a negative air pressure and you do not have enough combustible air in the house.

The easiest way to alleviate that is to install one of those air-to-air systems that draws air directly into the furnace's cold air return. This will increase the amount of air in the burner of your home's furnace and let it function more efficiently. They only cost around $90 and should eliminate your condensation problem.

If you want, you can also solve the problem by buying one of the more sophisticated air filter systems by Skuttle.

WINNING THE COLD WAR

THE ULTRASONIC SOLUTION

100 How Do I Solve the Dust Problem on My Ultrasonic Humidifier?

Materials needed: Demineralizing System.

Ultrasonic humidifiers produce a fine white dust from the minerals inside the tap water we use to fill the humidifier. To solve the problem just go to your local hardware store and buy a demineralizing system that hooks on to the water spout in your kitchen. This filter will take the minerals out of the water when you fill your humidifier.

101 Is There Any Maintenance I Should Do on My Ultrasonic Humidifier?

Materials needed: C W 16 (TM)

Your Ultrasonic Humidifier just about takes care of itself. You just have to change the filters and clean the water tank.

Cleaning the water tank every week or so is very important. Some people make the mistake of cleaning the tank with bleach or putting an additive in the water. These are definite "No No's". Bleach is very corrosive and will ruin your plastic water tank. Water additives have an oil base that will give the ultrasonic mist an oily consistency that you will not like in the house. The use of additives should only be considered in places that have an extremely high mineral content in their water.

Instead, pick up a product called C W 16 (TM) by the Twin Oaks People. this is an organic de-limer that will keep your tank gunk-free. You can also use it to clean the tray in your furnace humidifier.

WINNING THE COLD WAR

102 What's New With Ultrasonics?

Ultrasonic humidifiers are going through a metamorphosis. Companies like Sunbeam, Holmes and Bionaire have been doing a great deal of research and really lifted the state of the art. If you are in the market for a new humidifier, there are two new types to look at.

Sunbeam has a warm air mist ultrasonic humidifier that almost eliminates the demineralizing of the water droplet. This new system adds a definite comfort factor and also solves the white dust problem.

The other new ultrasonic humidifiers we're seeing on the market are using what we call "coated transducers". This also attacks the gray mist problem. These new ultrasonics put a dimineralizing filter in line that you change once or twice a season depending on water hardness. They also give you a litmus paper to test the water hardness and determine how often the filter needs to be changed.

WINNING THE COLD WAR

103 What Do You Think About the Enviracaire Air Cleaner?

The Enviracaire EV-1 is still the Cadillac of the field. It is a dual air filter air cleaner, with a charcoal wrapper and a H.E.P.A. filter that clears the majority of dust, pollen, even radon gas from the air in your home.

The Enviracaire EV-1 will clear about 18,000 cubic feet of air. One unit can easily keep a 1,200 square foot ranch clean. It's prime location should be in the largest room in the house, but since it is completely portable it can be moved from room to room if necessary. If you have a two story home, I recommend two units, one on each floor.

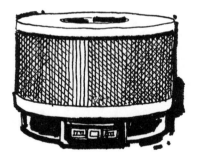

WINNING THE COLD WAR

104 I Enclosed My Furnace When I Refinished My Basement. What Do I Do to Make Sure My Furnace Is Getting Enough Air?

Materials needed: Cold Air Return Vent.

Equipment needed: Saw

Your furnace is extremely strong on the draw cycle and it will draw air right through your window frames and door openings. The coldest and heaviest air in a room is near the floor.

To make certain your furnace is getting enough air, cut a cold air return in the bottom of the wall closest to the furnace. Then check upstairs to make certain that you don't have furniture or draperies cutting off the cold air returns in the rest of the house.

The majority of the air comes from the cold air return system. As long as you are not blocking those, your furnace will do fine.

105 What's Wrong With My Furnace? Whenever My Furnace Comes on There Is a Damp, Musty Smell.

There is nothing wrong with your furnace. The problem is that your basement is too damp. When your furnace comes on, the first air it pulls in is from the basement cold air return. If that air is damp and musty, it retains the smell when your furnace heats it and sends the smell upstairs.

WINNING THE COLD WAR

106 I'm Buying a New Furnace. My Old Furnace Is About 30 Years Old, So I've Been Out of the Market for a While. Should I Choose a 70%, 80% or 90% Efficient Furnace?

Good Question. Older furnaces at their best were only about 40% efficient. That means that if we took our heating dollar, 60% of it was being wasted and going up the chimney every time you turned on your furnace. Only 40 cents of your dollar was actually going into heating your house.

If you go up to an 80% efficient furnace, 8 dimes are going into heating your house, 2 dimes are going up the chimney. If you go into a 90% efficient furnace, 9 dimes are being used for heat, and only one dime is gong up the chimney.

That would make it seem like the 90% efficient furnace was a better buy. However, if the difference in price between the 80 and the 90% efficient furnace is between $700 and $1,000, the 90% efficient furnace is not a good buy. I would buy the 80% efficient furnace, put a little extra insulation into the ceiling of my house, and pocket the difference.

If the difference between the 80 and 90% efficient furnace is only $300, I would probably take the 90% efficient one. I'd still probably spend a couple of hundred dollars on some extra insulation into the ceiling of my home.

WINNING THE COLD WAR

107 I've Just Had a 90% Efficient Furnace Installed. What Should I Do to Make Certain That It Is Getting Enough Air to Be Operating Efficiently?

You shouldn't have to do a thing. Unlike other furnaces, when you go up to a 90% efficient furnace it no longer relies on your chimney and the cold air return system that was built into your house. Instead they install an air source PVC pipe.

When your heating contractor installs a 90% efficient furnace he is also supposed to install this special air return system.

In what looks like a one pipe system, there are two channels inside the pipe. The inside channel is the air intake channel. The outside channel is the exhaust channel.

ODD JOBS
Chapter IX

ODD JOBS

108 What's the Best Way to Clear the Drain Hole in the Back of My Frost Free Refrigerator?

Materials needed: Hot Water

Equipment needed: Baster

Joe Gagnon, the Appliance Doctor, at Carmack Appliance in Garden City, Michigan, gave me an instant solution to this problem.

In the back wall of the refrigerator is a drain hole. Take the baster you use for your turkey and fill it full of hot water. Wrap a small piece of rag around the tip of the baster and shove the baster tip tightly into the hole.

Now squeeze the bulb full of hot water down into the hole. The combination of the heat and the hot water will flush away whatever is plugging the hole.

Joe says that it is very important NOT TO DO ANYTHING ELSE. The plastic drain tube is very delicate and sticking a metal darning needle, or using something like ammonia, bleaches or lyes, will do a great deal of damage.

Remember: use hot water only. The fast results will amaze you. After you've cleared the clog, empty the drain pan from underneath the refrigerator. Dust and scrub the area, and the pan. Put some baking soda into the drain pan when you replace it. That will keep it clean and fresh smelling.

ODD JOBS

109 Every 10 or 15 Minutes the Water Tank on the Commode Flushes All by Itself. How Do I tell what's wrong?

Materials needed: Food coloring

First do a food coloring water test. Take a bottle of food coloring into the bath room. Take the lid off the water tank. Flush the toilet.

After the tank has emptied and is beginning to refill pour some food coloring into the holding tank. Put the lid back on the tank and go away for ten minutes.

When you come back ten minutes later, lift the seat of the commode. If you can see the food coloring in the bowl, you need to replace the flapper ball.

FOOD COLORING

ODD JOBS

110 How Do I Stop the Water From Leaking in the Water Closet of My Commode?

Materials needed: Flapper Ball and Epoxy Gasket Kit.

Take the top off the tank and check to see if the flapper ball fits snugly. If it does, then the flapper ball is OK and you have to replace the gasket.

If the gasket is nice and smooth, then you have to replace the flapper ball.

When you go to buy a replacement, it's important to bring the name of the water closet, because sizes are not uniform, and many different brands have different sizes. Once you buy the right size flapper ball, the rest is easy. There are very good directions in every kit. Just follow the direction, and you should be done in four minutes or less.

ODD JOBS

111 How Do I Stop Noise in My Water Pipes?

Noisy water pipes are a sign that the "air chamber" in the pipes has been disrupted and a partial vacuum has formed. This vacuum causes the pipes to shake. You don't need a plumber. This six step procedure can silence them easily.

1 Check all the toilets to be sure they're full. Then turn off the water valves leading to each toilet.

2 Turn off the main shut-off valve by the water meter.

3 Turn on the cold water faucets that are farthest away and closest to the water meter. Drain all the cold water from the pipes.

4 Next, close the two faucets.

5 Re-open the main shut-off, and open the valves on the toilets.

6 Turning the cold water faucets on and off a few times will establish a new air chamber and silence the noise.

ODD JOBS

112 My Hot Water Smells Like Rotten Eggs. What Do I Do?

Materials needed: Aluminum Anode Rod

First, check behind the drapes to make sure the kids didn't miss an Easter egg.

Seriously, thanks to Jim Kronk of Universal Plumbing, I can tell you that the probable cause of the rotten egg smell in your hot water is that you have a sulphur build-up in your hot water tank.

This is not a problem in most large cities. However, in areas where there is a high mineral content in the well water, the problem is caused by the magnesium anode rod in the hot water tank.

When this problem occurs, it is usually solved by getting an aluminum anode rod from the local plumbing supply and replacing the magnesium rod in their tank. This will change the PH factor in the water and eliminate the problem. It will also make the hot water tank last a great deal longer. Complete directions will come with the replacement anode rod.

It is a good idea to replace the anode rod in all hot water heaters every five or six years.

ODD JOBS

113 How Do I Tell if I Need a Dehumidifier in My Basement?

Materials needed: Mil-Du-Gas® Bag, Newspaper, 2′ X 2′ Piece of Reynolds Wrap (TM), Tape

You can get rid of the "moldy" smell with a Mil-Du-Gas® Bag from your local hardware store or home center.

To test if you have a moisture problem in the basement, put a couple of sheets of newspaper on the floor. Cover the newspaper with aluminum foil which is then taped to the floor.

Let the foil-newspaper package stand for two days. Lift it up. If the newspaper is wet, you have water or moisture coming from the floor.

If the aluminum foil is fogged on top, you're going to have the "musties", and a dehumidifier is in order.

If the paper is wet, start by redirecting exterior water run off and improve the slope of the terrain away from the house.

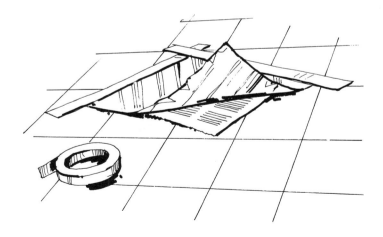

ODD JOBS

114 How Do I Bring Back the Shine to My Aluminum Storm Doors?

Materials needed: Parker & Bailey Stainless Steel Polish

Equipment needed: Cotton Rags

Aluminum is a real problem for anyone who doesn't want to use an acid based cleaner. Storm doors get especially dingy during the winter when water based cleaners just freeze. Homemakers have discovered this tip and passed it on to me. You can use it on both painted and non painted aluminum.

Pour a small amount of Parker & Bailey (called F. O. Bailey in some parts of the country) Stainless Steel Polish on a rag. Apply it to a small section of the door and then buff with another cotton rag. The polish will not only clean off all the fingerprints and dulling, air borne contaminants, but leave behind a hard protecting finish that will preserve the shine for a long time. The product is non abrasive, so it will not scratch.

Try the same technique on any interior or exterior aluminum or steel surface. You will be impressed with the results.

ODD JOBS

115 How Do You Make Doorwall Tracks Run Smooth?

Materials needed: Ammonia Style Window Cleaner, White Lithium Grease

Equipment needed: Vacuum Cleaner with Crevice Tool, Cotton Rags, Stiff Old Paint Brush.

The aluminum tracks for doorwalls and windows can get so clogged that they become almost impossible to open and close.

1 Clear all the loose particles with a vacuum cleaner and crevice tool.

2 Clean the tracks thoroughly with an ammonia style window cleaner like Windex with Ammonia. Use an old 2" stiff bristled paint brush to get into all the cracks and cervices. Wipe up with a cotton rag.

3 Get some White Lithium Grease at a hardware, auto supply store or home center. Apply a small amount to a rag and put a thin coat on the tracks. Use White Lithium Grease only. No substitutes. This highly specialized product is not effected by cold or heat and will keep your doorwalls and windows running smoothly.

Repeat the process on the upper tracks.

While you're at it, check the guide wheels for wear. If the wheels bind, replace them. Replacement parts are readily available in the door hardware department of any good hardware store or home center.

APPENDIX

HOW TO FIND IT

Here is a sellection of my most asked phone numbers. If you can't find what you're looking for at your local home center or hardware store, don't dispair. Look up the brand name and then call the parent company. They'll be glad to tell you where to find what you need.

PRODUCT	COMPANY	PHONE
Air Bear Air Cleaners	Trion Corp.	800-338-7466
Air Duct Cleaning	Air Duct Clners Assoc	202-737-2926
Andersen Windows	Anderson Window Corp.	800-426-4261
Antique Oil Finish	Minwax Company Inc.	800-462-0194
Armorall	Armorall Home Co.	800-398-3892
B-I-N Primer Sealer	William Zinsser & Co.	908-469-8100
Bamboo Flooring	Smith & Fong Co.	415-285-8230
Bar Keepers Friend	Servaas Laboratories	800-433-5818
Bathtub Liners	Re Bath Company	800-426-4573
Benjamin Moore Paints	Benjamin Moore	800-344-0400
Bionaire Humidifiers	Bionaire Corporation	800-253-2764
BIX Driveway Cleaner	BIX Manufacturing	800-251-1098
BIX Paint Remover	BIX Manufacturing	800-251-1098
Bon Ami	Bon Ami	816-842-1230
Bondex Flooring	Bondex International	800-231-6781
Brite Ceramic Tile Cleaner	S.C. Johnson Wax	800-558-5252
Bruce Hardwood Flooring	Bruce	800-722-4647
Bryant Heating & Cooling	Bryant	800-428-4326
Bug Stuff	Atlanta Sundries	800-253-3957
Cabot Wood Care Products	Samuel Cabot	800-877-8246
Carrier Heating & Cooling	Carrier	800-227-7437
Cement & Concrete Patch	Quikrete	800-282-5828
Cetol DEK	Akzo Nobel Coatings	800-833-7288
Chair Loc	Chair Loc Company	908-657-4501
Citra-Solv	Bio Wash	800-663-9274
Citristrip	Specialty Environmental	800-899-0401
Clean Away	Orange Sol	800-877-7771
Clear Magic	Westley's Blue Coral	800-545-0982
Clear Solutions	Samuel Cabot	800-877-8246

PRODUCT	COMPANY	PHONE
Cobra Ridge Vent	GAF Materials	800-688-6654
Combo Vent	Combo Vent Company	800-298-7610
Comfort Base	Homasote Company	800-257-9491
Coronodo Cement Stain	Coronado Paints	800-883-4193
Counter Polish	Hopes Counter Top Polish	800-325-4026
Cove Master	Tapco International	800-521-8486
Crystal II	Fabulon	800-876-7005
CWF-UV	Flood Company	800-321-3444
Danish Oil	Deft Inc.	800-544-3338
Dap Life Premium	Dap Inc.	800-327-3339
Dap Wood Filler	Dap Inc.	800-327-3339
De-Solv-It	Orange Sol	800-877-7771
Decking	Brock Dock	800-365-3625
Diamond Brite Sealant	Diamond Brite	800-334-8388
Dif Wall Paper Remover	William Zinsser & Co.	908-469-8100
Dirtex	Savogran Company	800-225-9872
DL Hand Cleaner	Loctite Corporation	800-243-4874
Dupont Corian	Dupont	800-426-7426
Duraseal	Minwax Company Inc.	800-462-0194
Dutch Boy Paints	Dutch Boy Paints	800-828-5669
Easi-Air Respirator	3 M	800-243-4630
Easy Mask	Daubert Coated Products	800-634-1303
Elmer's Carp. Wood Glue	Elmer's Adhesives	800-848-9400
Enviracaire EV-1	Environmental Air Cntrl.	800-332-1110
Face Lift	Thompson & Formby	800-367-6297
Famowood	Beverly Mfg Co.	800-933-3211
Fiba Tape	Bay Mills Ltd	800-762-6694
Firma Bond	ABC Supply Co.	313-846-0600
Fix & Patch	Darworth Co	800-624-7767
Foam Off	Bio Wash	800-663-9274
Fresh Air Paint	Kurfees Coatings	800-626-5244
Furniture Face Lift	Thompson & Formby	800-367-6297
Garage Doors	Overhead Door Corp	800-543-2269
Garage Doors	Raynor Garage Doors	800-472-9667
Garage Doors	Roll-Tite Overhead Door	800-959-9559

PRODUCT	COMPANY	PHONE
Garage Doors	Stanley Doors	800-521-2752
Garage Doors	Wayne-Dalton	800-827-3667
Gel Gloss	TR Industries	310-923-0838
Gelled Wood Stain	Wood-Kote Products	800-843-7666
Go Jo Hand Cleaner	Go Jo Industries	800-321-9647
Goo Gone	Magic American	800-321-6330
Goof Off	Atlanta Sundries	800-253-3957
Graffiti Removal	BCD International	800-772-9339
Great Stuff	Insta Foam Products	800-800-3626
Gym Seal	McCloskey	800-345-4530
H2 Oil Base Stain Kill	William Zinser	908-469-8100
Hartco Touch Up Kit	Hartco	800-4HARTCO
Heil Heating & Cooling	Inter City Products	800-458-6650
Holmes Humidifiers	Holmes Air	800-546-5637
Home Security	Home Automation Labs	800-229-7256
Honeywell Magistat	Honeywell	800-328-5111
Hopes Counter Polish	Hopes	800-325-4026
Hunter Thermostats	Hunter Fan Co	901-743-1360
Int. Storm Window Kits	Window Saver Co.	800-321-9276
Invisible Shield	Unelko Corporation	800-528-3149
Kilz And Kilz II	Masterchem Industries	800-325-3552
Kover Stain	William Zinsser & Co.	908-469-8100
Krebs Paint Sprayers	Krebs Inc	800-525-6067
Lennox Heating & Cooling	Lennox Industries	214-497-5000
Lexell Crystal Clear Calk	Sashco Sealants	800-767-5656
Lift Off # 1,2,3,4, & 5	Motsenbocker's	800-346-1633
Liquid Sandpaper	General Liquids Corp.	410-484-7222
Loctite	Loctite Corporation	800-243-4874
Meguiar's #2	Meguiars Inc.	800-347-5700
Meguiar's Swirl Remover	Meguiars Inc.	800-347-5700
Mil Du Gas Bags	Star Brite Corp.	800-327-8583
Mildew Stain Remover	Magic American Corp	800-321-6330
Minwax Woodcare Products	Minwax Company	800-462-0194
Mr. Long Arm	Diamond Brite	800-334-8388
Mr. Mac's Concrete Products	Macklanburg-Duncan	800-654-8454

PRODUCT	COMPANY	PHONE
Nice N Easy	Alumin-Nu	800-899-7097
Non Metal Steel Wool Pads	3 M	800-364-3577
Nu-Finish	Reed Union Corp.	800-877-7771
Old Hard Adhesive Remover	Tile Helper	708-453-6900
Olympic Wood Sealer	Ppg Industries	800-441-9695
One Time	Red Devil	800-423-3845
Orange-Sol	Orange-Sol Inc.	800-877-7771
Pacific Strong	Bona Kemi Usa	800-872-5515
Parker & Bailey Cleaners	Imperial Mfg.	312-243-1112
Pattern Plus	Hartco	800-4HARTCO
PBC Deglosser	Savogran Company	800-225-9872
Pella Windows & Doors	Pella Corp	800-847-3552
Penofin	Performance Coatings	800-468-8820
Perma-White Paint	William Zinsser & Co.	908-469-8100
Plastic Laminates	Formica Corp	800-524-0159
Pond Restorer	Alumin-Nu Corp	800-899-7097
Power	Alumin-Nu Corp.	800-899-7097
Pro Mesh	Custom Tapes Company	800-621-7994
Procelain Crack Repair	Nuporce Products	800-994-9970
Quick Tite	Loctite Corporation	800-243-4874
Rag Roller	Detroit Quality Brush	800-722-3037
Rain X	Unelko Corporation	800-528-3149
Red Stain Off	Harvard Chemical	800-423-7514
Reem Heating & Cooling	Reem Air Conditioners	501-646-4311
Renovator	Minwax Company	800-462-0194
Respirator Dust/Mist	3 M	800-364-3577
Restorex Wood Cleaner	Surco Products	800-556-0111
Roofing & Insulation	Owens-Corning	800-438-7465
Roofing & Ventilation	Certain Teed Corp	800-345-1145
Rubbol Dek	Akzo Nobel Coatings	800-833-7288
Rudd Heating & Cooling	Rudd Air Conditioners	501-646-4311
Safe & Simple	Carver Tripp (Parks)	800-225-8543
Safety Goggles	3 M	612-737-6586
Scald Safe Adapter	Resources Conservation	800-243-2862
Scotchtint UV Film	3 M	800-364-3577

PRODUCT	COMPANY	PHONE
Seasonite	Flood Company	800-321-3444
Sherwin Williams Paints	Sherwin-Williams	800-424-5837
Shingle Shield	Chicago Metallic	800-323-7164
Sikkens Wood Care Products	Akzo Nobel Coatings	800-833-7288
Simple Deck	Bio Wash	800-663-9274
Simple Green	Sunshine Makers	800-228-0709
Skuttle Model 16	Skuttle Mfg	800-848-9786
Soft Scrub	Clorox Company	800-537-2823
Space Pak	Mestek Company	413-568-9571
Square Buff Sander	Flecto Co.	800-635-3286
Squeak Ender	E & E Engineering	800-854-3577
Sta-Clean Mildicide Add.	Envirochem	800-247-9011
Street Shoe Wood Finish	Basic Coatings	800-247-5471
Strip Ease	Savogran Company	800-225-9872
Sun Pipe	Sun Pipe Company	800-844-4786
Sunbeam Humidifiers	Sunbeam Housewares	800-597-5978
Super Mildex	Atlanta Sundries	800-253-3957
Super Strip	Savogran Company	800-225-9872
Thompson's Wd. Protector	Thompson & Formby	800-367-6297
Thompson's Wood Sealer	Thompson & Formby	800-367-6297
Time Tracker	RBC Safe & Secure	800-331-2030
Trane Heating & Cooling	Trane Company	800-445-6573
Transparent Coatings	Waterlox Chemicals	800-321-0377
Trex Wood Composite	Mobil Chemical Co.	800-289-8739
Trion Max 4 & 5	Trion Corp.	800-338-7466
TSP	Savogran Company	800-225-9872
Unilock Pavers	Unilock Pavers	800-864-5625
VOC Varathane	Flecto Co.	800-635-3286
Wagner Presure Sprayers	Wagner Spray Tech.	800-328-8251
Wash Before You Paint	Cul-Mac Industries	800-626-5089
Watco	Flecto Co.	800-635-3286
Water Powered Sump Pump	Zoelar Corporation	800-928-7867
Water Seal Ultra	Thompson & Formby	800-367-6297
Waterlox Transparent	Waterlox Chemicals	800-321-0377
Weathergard Sealer	Protek Pavers	800-992-7425

PRODUCT	COMPANY	PHONE
Westley's Clear Magic	Mckay Chemical Co.	**800-446-2529**
Wolman Toner & Sealers	Wolman Products	**800-556-7737**
Wood Flooring Dist.	Erickson's Flooring	**800-225-9663**
Wood Patch	United Gilsonite Labs	**800-845-5227**
Wood Stain & Wood Filler	Basic Coatings	**800-247-5471**
Wood Stains	Cupernol Stains	**800-424-5837**
Works Bath & Shwr. Clnr.	Lime 0 Sol Co.	**219-587-9151**
X-10 Home Security	X-10 (USA)	**201-784-9700**
X-14	Block Drug Co.	**800-365-6500**
X-I-M Stain Kills	X-I-M Products	**800-262-8469**
York Heating & Cooling	York International	**717-771-6418**
Zip Strip	Star Bronze Co.	**800-327-8583**
Zip-Guard Finish	Star Bronze Co.	**800-321-9870**
Zone Heat Controls	Duro Dyne Midwest	**800-966-6446**

INDEX

Learn How To *Paint it Inside:*

Take the Pain out of Painting -Interiors- by Glenn Haege

ISBN 1-880615-19-3
$14.97

Even people who have been painting for twenty years or more tell America's Master Handyman, Glenn Haege, that they started painting faster, easier, and with better, more professional results after reading this book.

The Bookwatch says:

"Finally: a guide to interior do-it-yourself painting which follows a very simple yet information packed step-by-step format!...A very basic, essential home reference."

The Detroit News says:

"Haege makes it easy for anyone smart enough to lift a paint can lid... to solve a particular painting problem."

This one, power packed book contains the information you need to have a great looking job every time.

This book will show you how to:
- **Prepare a room so well you may not need to paint.**
- **Remove wallpaper and peeling paint easily and prepare a firm painting foundation.**
- **Paint even slippery surfaces like kitchen cabinets.**
- **Use special Stain Kill Paints to solve *impossible* painting problems.**
- **Make paint look like wallpaper, wood, and stone, in a fabulous 40 page "Faux Finish" section.**
- **Plus Much, Much More.**

Fast & Easy! © 1995 MHP

Outside:

Take the Pain out of Painting -Exteriors- by Glenn Haege

Your home's exterior paint is all that protects your family's largest single investment from the elements. America's master handyman, Glenn Haege, shows you the easy, economical ways to give your house the protection it deserves.

ISBN 1-880615-15-0
$12.95

George Hampton of *The Booklist* says:
"Writing for paint retailers, contractors, and homeowners alike, Haege vends plenty of practical information organized into step-by-step procedures for everything"

Hormer Formby, the originator of Formby Finishes says:
"Glenn Haege knows more about Paints and Products than anybody I have ever known."

This book will show you how to:
- **Get the most for your painting dollar.**
- **Choose a painting contractor.**
- **Get rid of mold and mildew.**
- **Prepare the surface so the paint will wear like iron.**
- **Paint wood, vinyl, aluminum, concrete, log, shingles and all other exterior surfaces.**
- **Varnish or revarnish a log cabin.**
- **Paint, stain, or varnish exterior toys and furniture.**
- **Plus Much Much More.**

Bring Back the Beauty to your Hardwood Floors.

If you are one of the millions who have just discovered hardwood floors underneath their carpeting, or are thinking about installing hardwood in your home, this book can be a real life saver.

Glenn Haege tells you all about hardwood, then gives four different ways to refinish floors, including one technique that will let you get the entire job done in a single day.

Glenn Haege's *Complete*
HARDWOOD FLOOR CARE GUIDE

How to Refinish & Care for Your Wood Floors

ISBN 1-880615-38-X
$6.95

This book will show you how to:
- **Save hundreds of dollars on hardwood or pine floor refinishing.**
- **Bring back the beauty to an old, lusterless wood floor in a single day.**
- **Get new, light weight equipment that makes it possible for any man or woman to refinish hardwood or pine floors.**
- **Decide which type of floor finish goes best with your life style.**
- **Select new, miracle finishes that are easy to apply, dry in hours, wear well and have almost no odor.**
- **Decide whether you want to wax or not wax your floors.**
- **Keep your floors looking their best.**
- **Solve all sorts of problems from bubbles and blisters to water and paint stains, even (ech) chewing gum.**
- **Live with, and love your hardwood floors.**

Vital, Need-to-Know Info
for Deck Owners

Whether you are one of the 30 million Americans who own a deck, or are one of the one million who will build a wood deck or paver patio this year, this guide contains vital, new research you won't find anwhere else.

USDA Forest Service research indicates former staining and sealing recommendations may be wrong. Canadian proprietary research indicates some of the most popular deck cleaners may actually damage decks.

ISBN 1-880615-40-1
$6.95

The TV commercials are very confusing. How are you supposed to know which products will do the best job on your deck or paver walk or patio? America's Master Handyman, Glenn Haege, has done the research and compiled easy to understand instructions for you.

Here's a list of some of the information in this guide:
- **How to decide whether a deck or paver patio is best for your lifestyle.**
- **The differences in deck woods that can save you thousands of dollars.**
- **How to keep pressure treated wood from splitting.**
- **How to cut through the confusion about sealers, toners, UV coatings and wood stains.**
- **How to create a "furniture finish" deck.**
- **Easy step by step instructions on deck & paver care.**
- **How to bring back the beauty to deck wood.**
- **How to make paver colors come alive.**
- **How to keep pavers looking beautiful and new.**

First Aid for your pocket book.

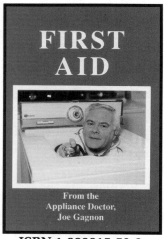

FIRST AID

From the
Appliance Doctor,
Joe Gagnon

ISBN 1-880615-50-9
$14.97

This book is for you if you would rather spend your money on a new cd player than replacing the garbage disposer.

You don't get any medals for repairing or replacing a major appliance. *Joe Gagnon* shows how to keep them running better, longer; how to repair them when they break, and how to cut through the hype when it comes time to buy new.

The Chicago Sun Times says:

"Many Home Owners will save money with a copy of *First Aid From the Appliance Doctor,* by Joseph Gagnon. They also could save some lives."

The Davis Enterprise says:

"To become empowered, read appliance doctor's book."

TWENTYONE Magazine says:

"The information is *First Aid* can save you money. It's a book every homeowner will want to keep on the reference shelf."

This book will show you how to:

- **Save hundreds of dollars on appliance purchase and repair.**
- **Cut through the lies in retail appliance ads.**
- **Tell the difference between a cheap promotional appliance and one that's built ot last.**
- **Make your appliances run better and last longer.**
- **Master the repairs you can easily do yourself.**
- **Keep from being ripped off on parts and service.**

TO: Master Handyman Press, Inc.
P.O. Box 1498
Royal Oak, MI. 48068-1498

Please send me copies of the following books:
All books are sold with a 100% money back, satisfaction guaranty:

__   **FIX IT FAST & EASY!**   @ $14.95 each = $_____
__   **TAKE THE PAIN OUT OF PAINTING!**
    - INTERIORS -   @ $14.97 each = $_____
__   **TAKE THE PAIN OUT OF PAINTING!**
    -EXTERIORS-   @ $12.95 each = $_____
__   **Glenn Haege's COMPLETE DECK &**
    PAVER CARE GUIDE   @ $ 6.95 each = $_____
__   **Glenn Haege's Complete HARDWOOD**
    FLOOR CARE GUIDE   @ $ 6.95 each = $_____
__   **FIRST AID from the Appliance Doctor,**
    Joe Gagnon   @ $14.97 each = $_____

Total $_____

Michigan Residents: Please add 6% Sales Tax.

Shipping: Surface $2.50 for the first book and $1 for each additional.
Air Mail: $3.50 per book.

SHIPPING: _____

Total $_____

Name: _____
Phone No _____
Address: _____
_____   ZIP:_____

Credit Card Information. Please fill out if you wish to charge.
Please charge my _____ Visa   _____ Master Card
Expiration Date: _____ Card #_____
Name on Card: _____
Signature: _____

Mail to:

Master Handyman Press, Inc.
P.O. Box 1498
Royal Oak, MI 48068-1498

TO: **Master Handyman Press, Inc.**
P.O. Box 1498
Royal Oak, MI. 48068-1498

Please send me copies of the following books:
All books are sold with a 100% money back, satisfaction guaranty:

__ **FIX IT FAST & EASY!**   @ **$14.95 each = $** _____
__ **TAKE THE PAIN OUT OF PAINTING!**
       - INTERIORS -   @ **$14.97 each = $** _____
__ **TAKE THE PAIN OUT OF PAINTING!**
       -EXTERIORS-   @ **$12.95 each = $** _____
__ **Glenn Haege's COMPLETE DECK &**
       PAVER CARE GUIDE   @ **$ 6.95 each = $** _____
__ **Glenn Haege's Complete HARDWOOD**
       FLOOR CARE GUIDE   @ **$ 6.95 each = $** _____
__ **FIRST AID from the Appliance Doctor,**
       Joe Gagnon   @ **$14.97 each = $** _____

                              Total $ _____

Michigan Residents: Please add 6% Sales Tax.

Shipping: Surface $2.50 for the first book and $1 for each additional.
Air Mail: $3.50 per book.

          SHIPPING: _____

                              Total $ _____
Name: _____
Phone No _____
Address: _____
_____ ZIP: _____

Credit Card Information. Please fill out if you wish to charge.
Please charge my _____ Visa   _____ Master Card
Expiration Date: _____ Card # _____
Name on Card: _____
Signature: _____

Mail to:

**Master Handyman Press, Inc.
P.O. Box 1498
Royal Oak, MI 48068-1498**